D1475563

NEW TURKISH CINEMA

TAURIS WORLD CINEMA SERIES

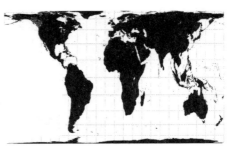

Series Editor: Lúcia Nagib
Advisory Board: Laura Mulvey (UK), Donald Richie (Japan), Robert Stam (USA), Ismail Xavier (Brazil)

The aim of the **Tauris World Cinema Series** is to reveal and celebrate the richness and complexity of film art across the globe. A wide variety of cinemas will be explored, both in the light of their own cultures and in the ways they interconnect with each other in a global context.

The books in the series will represent innovative scholarship, in tune with the multicultural character of contemporary audiences and designed to appeal to both the film expert and the general interest reader. It will draw upon an international authorship, comprising academics, film writers and journalists.

Prominent strands of the series will include **World Film Theory**, offering new theoretical approaches as well as re-assessments of major movements, filmmakers, genres, technologies and stars; **New Cinemas,** focusing on recent film revivals in different parts of the world; and **new translations** into English of international milestones of film theory and criticism.

Books in the series include:

Brazil on Screen: Cinema Novo, New Cinema, Utopia
Lucia Nagib

East Asian Cinemas: Exploring Transnational Connections on Film
Edited by Leon Hunt and Leung Wing-Fai

Lebanese Cinema: Imagining the Civil War and Beyond
Lina Khatib

Contemporary New Zealand Cinema: From New Wave to Blockbuster
Edited by Ian Conrich and Stuart Murray

On Cinema
Glauber Rocha, edited by Ismail Xavier, translated by Stephanie Dennison

Queries, ideas and submissions to:
Series Editor, Professor Lúcia Nagib – l.nagib@leeds.ac.uk
Cinema Editor at I.B. Tauris, Philippa Brewster – p.brewster@blueyonder.co.uk

NEW TURKISH CINEMA

BELONGING, IDENTITY
AND MEMORY

Asuman Suner

I.B. TAURIS

LONDON · NEW YORK

Published in 2010 by I.B.Tauris & Co Ltd
6 Salem Road, London W2 4BU
175 Fifth Avenue, New York NY 10010
www.ibtauris.com

Distributed in the United States and Canada Exclusively by Palgrave Macmillan,
175 Fifth Avenue, New York NY 10010

ISBN 978 1 84511 949 2 (HB)
       978 1 84511 950 8 (PB)

A full CIP record for this book is available from the British Library
A full CIP record is available from the Library of Congress

Library of Congress Catalog Card Number: available

Typeset by JCS Publishing Services Ltd, www.jcs-publishing.co.uk

Printed and bound in India by Thomson Press India Ltd

To my Tuna

CONTENTS

ILLUSTRATIONS

ACKNOWLEDGMENTS

My work on new wave Turkish cinema has grown over a span of many years. There are many individuals who have contributed to this project in various ways. I would like to thank Ackbar Abbas, Meltem Ahıska, Ayşe Gül Altınay, Jülide Aksiyote, Caroline Anderson, Pelin Aytemiz, Gülsüm Baydar, Chris Berry, Barton Byg, Can Candan, Shohini Chaudhuri, Feride Çiçekoğlu, Banu Göknar, Erdağ Göknar, Deniz Göktürk, Faik Gür, Ahmet Gürata, Güven Güzeldere, Sibel Irzık, Özlem Köksal, Dilek Kaya Mutlu, Hamid Naficy, Leyla Neyzi, Ayşe Öncü, Esra Özyürek, Boerte Sagaste, Gulschen Sahatova, Semih Sökmen, Halide Velioğlu, Zafer Yenal, and Fırat Yücel for their help and contribution at different stages of the work. This list also includes Özlem Okur, who unfortunately has passed away too early.

I am grateful to Nuri Bilge Ceylan, Zeki Demirkubuz, Eylem Kaftan, Tayfun Pirselimoğlu, Yeşim Ustaoğlu, and Derviş Zaim, who generously gave of their precious time to answer my questions.

Last but not least, I am indebted to Philippa Brewster, Nina Ergin, and Başak Ertur for both institutional and technical support. Without their professionalism and expertise, this book would not have been published.

INTRODUCTION

NEW TURKISH CINEMA IN HISTORICAL PERSPECTIVE

In one scene in *Toss Up* (*Yazı/Tura*, Uğur Yücel, 2004), the war veteran protagonist looks at the cave houses of his hometown Göreme after a night of heavy drinking and says in bewilderment: 'There are ghosts in these houses.' This line can be taken to express the central problem of the new wave Turkish cinema that emerged during the second half of the 1990s. New wave Turkish films, popular and art films alike, revolve around the figure of a 'spectral home.' Again and again they return to the idea of home/homeland; they reveal tensions, anxieties, and dilemmas around the questions of belonging, identity, and memory in contemporary Turkish society.

The figure of the spectral home at the center of new wave Turkish films might take on different forms and meanings. At times, it turns into a romantic fantasy of belonging, an idealized home that one nostalgically remembers and longs for. At other times, it becomes a haunted house. New wave Turkish cinema often tells us stories of uncanny houses haunted by the ghosts of the past – houses associated with trauma, violence, and horror.

I

The beginnings of cinema in Turkey date back to the late 1890s, when private screenings were held in the palace for the sultan's

1

court. The first movie theater was established in 1908 in Pera – the most cosmopolitan district of Istanbul – by Sigmund Weinberg, a Polish Jew from Romania. This was followed by several other theaters, mostly run by members of the non-Muslim minorities.

In terms of film production, the origins of Turkish cinema are quite puzzling. According to a generally held view among Turkish film critics, the first film by an Ottoman citizen was a documentary, *The Demolition of the Russian Monument at San Stefano* (*Ayastefanos Abidesinin Yıkılışı*), made in 1914 by Fuat Uzkınay, an army officer who had taken an interest in cinematography. However, this film did not survive; in fact, it is unclear whether it ever existed (Erdoğan and Göktürk, 2001: 534).[1] Moreover, several documentary films had already been made within the borders of the Ottoman Empire prior to 1914. Yet, most of these films have been excluded from Turkish film history because the filmmakers were not of Muslim-Turkish origin,[2] or because their identity was not known (Kaya Mutlu, 2007: 82).

During the final years of the empire, a handful of fiction films, mostly adaptations from theater or literature, were produced.[3] The period following the establishment of the Republic – that is, the years between 1923 and 1939 – has been designated the 'stage artists' era' in Turkish film history (Özön, 1995). Muhsin Ertuğrul, a reputed theater actor and director, almost exclusively dominated the cinema of the newly founded Republic. The films made in this period were often adapted from stage dramas or from films made in Europe and America. They are characterized by an exaggerated mode of acting and theatrical *mise-en-scène*.

The 1940s are often called a 'transition era' by film historians, since they represent a transition from a theater-oriented approach to a more cinematic style. During this era, directors without prior experience in theater started to make films. Several production companies were also established in these years.

In 1948, the municipal tax on domestic films was reduced to 25 percent (while the tax on foreign films remained 70 percent). Protecting Turkish cinema in financial terms, this regulation gave a boost to the commercial film industry. Thereafter, cinema began to emerge as a truly popular form of entertainment in Turkey during the 1950s.

A crucial decade in the history of modern Turkey, the 1950s were characterized by the transition from a single-party regime to multi-party democracy. The 1950 elections resulted in the victory of the Democratic Party over the Republican People's Party, which had been established by Mustafa Kemal Atatürk, the founder and first president of the Republic. In contrast to the elitist stance of the Republican People's Party, the Democratic Party emphasized populism and the rule of the people. The 1950s were a period of fast economic growth, industrialization and urbanization. It was also a time of increasing mass migration from the countryside to the cities, most notably to Istanbul. In this social and political climate, popular cinema began to flourish (Büker, 2002). With the 1948 tax reduction on domestic films, the film business was now open to anyone who sought profit (Erdoğan and Göktürk, 2001). Despite the increasing commercialization of the film sector, the 1950s also saw the emergence of several important filmmakers who developed their own cinematic style. Ömer Lütfi Akad, Metin Erksan, Atıf Yılmaz, Memduh Ün, Nejat Saydam, and Osman Seden are among the prominent directors of this period.

After its first beginnings in the 1950s, popular cinema had its heyday during the 1960s and early 1970s. The popular Turkish cinema of this period is generally called 'Yeşilçam cinema' (literally, pine-tree cinema), after the street in Istanbul where the film production companies were located. The period was characterized by a dizzying pace of film production. Increasing demand from the audience caused rapid expansion; during its golden years, 200 films were produced every year on average (Büker, 2002). These films entertained not only domestic audiences, but also became popular in other Middle Eastern countries such as Iran, Iraq, and Egypt (Erdoğan, 1998). This period also generated a unique mode of production, essentially determined by regional distributors. Typically, producers contacted the regional film distributors in provincial towns to negotiate plots and stars. Knowing their audience's tastes, the distributors could demand revisions to plot and casting (Erdoğan and Göktürk, 2001). While melodrama and comedy were the prominent genres of Yeşilçam cinema, historical action adventure or gangster movies were also produced. Mainly a cinema of stars, Yeşilçam did not grant much power to directors. Despite all these adverse factors, directors such as Duygu Sağıroğlu, Ertem Göreç, Halit Refiğ, Muharrem Gürses, Orhan Elmas, and Süreyya Duru, along with the veteran directors of the previous decade, made films in a coherent style, while working within the constraints of a highly commercialized industry. Films dealing with social issues – such as workers' rights, internal migration, and feudal relations – also began to appear in the 1960s. The most significant international success of Turkish cinema during this period was the Golden Bear awarded to Metin Erksan's *Dry Summer* (*Susuz Yaz*, 1963) at the 1964 Berlin Film Festival. Shot in a realist style, Erksan's film was about the conflicts surrounding ownership of land and water in southern Anatolia.

A period of great social and political upheaval as a result of continuous clashes between leftist and rightist groups, the 1970s witnessed the emergence of a politicized social-realist cinema in Turkey, mostly associated with the legendary director Yılmaz Güney. Güney entered the film business in the late 1950s, as a scriptwriter and production assistant. Shortly thereafter, he made his debut as an actor and quickly became very popular, particularly in the provinces. His appeal as an actor was linked to the rough anti-hero image that he created on screen, a sharp contrast to the polished images of the middle-class heroes dominating Turkish melodrama and romantic comedies at

4

the time. His natural acting style, which allowed him to bring elements from his own lower-class background to the screen, was greatly appreciated by the audience. His rude and upright tough-guy image earned him the nickname 'Ugly King' of Turkish cinema and quickly made him Turkey's most popular star in the mid-1960s. At that time, he starred in about twenty films per year, most of which were gangster films. Güney made his directorial debut in 1966; his early films followed the formula of the crime thrillers that had made him a star. It was not until the early 1970s that Güney began to make political films dealing with social problems in a realist style. He made his first political film, *Hope* (*Umut*), in 1970 – a milestone in Turkish cinema. In a peculiar realist style, *Hope* tells the story of an impoverished, naive horse-cab driver duped into searching for buried treasure. In 1972, Güney was arrested for sheltering anarchist refugees and sentenced to seven years in prison. He was pardoned and released in 1974 under a general amnesty. In the same year, however, he was again imprisoned, this time for murder.[4] Following his second imprisonment, he began to write detailed scripts in prison, to be filmed by his assistants. *The Herd* (*Sürü*, 1978), *The Enemy* (*Düşman*, 1979), and *The Way* (*Yol*, 1982) were written by Güney in prison and directed by Zeki Ökten (*The Herd* and *The Enemy*) and Şerif Gören (*The Way*) on his behalf.

Bringing Yılmaz Güney the Palme d'Or at the 1982 Cannes Film Festival,[5] *The Way* is arguably the most internationally acclaimed Turkish film ever made to date. Tracing the stories of five prisoners traveling on a week's leave from prison to different parts of Turkey, *The Way* presents a subtle critique of the 1980 military intervention. Each prisoner travels to a different part of eastern Anatolia to visit his family and resolve personal matters. The prisoners' hope and optimism quickly give way to desperation, as they find out that the 'free' society they are supposed to enter is no less claustrophobic and oppressive than prison. Using prison as a metaphor for the state of Turkish society under military rule, the film raises a radical critique not only of the oppressive Turkish state, but also of feudal traditions prevailing in rural Turkey. *The Way* is a legendary film in Turkey because of the extraordinary conditions under which it was produced: as mentioned above, Güney wrote the screenplay while in prison, in 1979. It was shot in the following year by his associate Şerif Gören.[6] Shortly thereafter, Güney escaped from prison and fled the country. In 1981, Güney himself edited the film in Switzerland and released it in Europe. After the film's success at Cannes in 1982, Güney completed his last film, *The Wall (Duvar,* 1983). He died of cancer in France in 1984, leaving not only more than a hundred films, but also innumerable stories about his charismatic personality, stormy relationships, political activities, and notorious temper.[7] Along with Güney's other films, *The Way* was banned in Turkey during the 1980s. It was not until the early 1990s that his films began to appear in theaters and on television. A group of directors – among them Ali Özgentürk, Bilge Olgaç, Erden Kıral, Ömer Kavur, Şerif Gören, Yavuz Özkan, Yusuf Kurçenli, and Zeki Ökten – who had either been associates of Yılmaz Güney or influenced by his cinema contributed to the development of the social-realist tradition during the 1970s and 1980s. Their films critically address social problems such as class inequality, social injustice, internal migration, economic underdevelopment, and feudal patriarchal relationships prevailing in rural Turkey. In the aftermath of the 1980 military coup, confronted with hardened censorship and a changing audience profile, the social-realist tradition gradually disappeared.

After its successful commercial growth from the 1950s to the mid-1970s, Turkish cinema started to decline in the late 1970s. The primary reason behind this decline was the paradoxical situation that, despite the commercial vitality of popular cinema, a powerful film industry never existed in Turkey. During the heyday of Yeşilçam cinema, profit-minded producers invested film revenues not in the film industry, but in other sectors in order to increase their personal wealth. As a result, while the commercial success of cinema made certain individuals rich, the foundations of the film industry remained vulnerable to fluctuations in the economy. The increasing production costs incurred through the transition to color cinematography, the political turmoil of the period (which prevented families from attending public events), and the nationwide expansion of television broadcasting had started to cause substantial financial problems for producers by the mid-1970s (Abisel, 1994). Having already lost most of its family audience by the late 1970s, Yeşilçam started to produce mainly soft-core pornographic films. In the early 1980s, the crisis in the film industry continued under the oppressive conditions created by the military regime.

The 12 September 1980 coup marks an important turning point in Turkey's recent history. The country's human rights record worsened gravely during this period. Following the coup, the military regime brought about a restructuring of the social and political institutions in accordance with the 1982 Constitution. Although a civil government took over in 1983, the authoritarian mentality behind the military-led 1982 Constitution has partly remained to this day. In terms of economy, the first half of the 1980s saw the introduction of a series of neo-liberal reforms – in particular, privatization and deregulation – counseled by the International Monetary Fund (IMF) under the patronage of the military government (Keyder, 1999). Also, a number of groundbreaking legal and technological reforms, particularly in the information and communication sectors, paved the way for Turkey's full integration into the global capitalist system. While enabling certain segments of Turkish society to become fully integrated into the globalizing world, rapid economic transformation also produced new forms of poverty. A widening income gap and social polarization created a picture of 'two Turkeys' that exist side by side, without much contact with each other (Keyder, 1999; Kandiyoti, 2002). Although the policy of systematic de-politicization pursued by the military regime was still effective, the mid-1980s witnessed the emergence of new social movements – including those of feminists, gay communities, and environmentalists – as well as new forms of social activism. Questions of cultural identity and difference became the yardstick of the new civil society movements of the period (Tekeli, 1995). Under the influence of the new social movements, the fundamental constituents of the Turkish Republic – that is, the principle of secularism, and a unified national identity – have undergone critical scrutiny since the second half of the 1980s (Kasaba, 1997).

In the oppressive political and social climate of the early 1980s, popular Turkish cinema became estranged from its traditional audience and could not keep pace with the trans-formation of society. Apart from a few successful films, the term 'Turkish film' turned into a joke, connoting bad taste and banality. In order to survive under these adverse conditions, film companies changed the medium and began to produce films in video format, targeting Turkish migrant workers in Europe. At the same time, filmmakers were trying to find new ways of expression, to address the changing dynamics of society. Different from the leftist social-realist perspective of the 1970s, films now centered on subjective issues. Under the influence of the powerful feminist movement of the period, one of the most frequently explored issues was the interroga-tion of female subjectivity and gender relations. A sub-genre called 'women's films' became popular during this period. Another emerging trend was the preoccupation with the possi-bilities of the medium itself. Self-reflexive films focused on the cinematic production process and problems of representation (Erdoğan and Göktürk, 2001).

The crisis in the film industry deepened throughout the 1980s and early 1990s. Not only did the number of the films produced drastically reduce, but so did the number of viewers. Atilla Dorsay (2004: 12), a prominent Turkish film critic, defines the early 1990s as the 'collapse of Turkish cinema' and points to developments in the culture industry as key factors behind this decline. These developments were related to the social and economic transformation of Turkey at the time. In economic terms, the period starting with the 1990s has been a period of perpetual crises for Turkey, during which the Turkish economy shrank significantly and investment declined, while bankruptcies and unemployment radically increased (Keyder, 2004). Despite these adverse factors, however, the 1990s have also been a decade of unprecedented expansion for the culture industry. As a result of neo-liberal policies of privatization and of opening up the domestic market to foreign investors, the media and advertising sectors have grown rapidly and boosted their profits. Advertising companies have established international connections and benefited from the expertise of the leading international brands in the sector (Erdoğan and Göktürk, 2001). Also, US distribution companies such as Warner Bros. and United International Pictures have opened branches in Turkey in order to take over the distribution of American films. These companies soon equipped their theaters with high-quality projection and sound systems. Now Turkish audiences can see Hollywood films at the same time as international audiences, as soon as they have been released, rather than having to wait months or even years.

Another key development was the commencement of private television. With the 1994 Code of Private Radio and Television Broadcasting, the monopoly of the state-based Turkish Radio and Television Institution (TRT) was officially terminated. The second half of the 1990s saw the emergence of hundreds of private radio stations and television channels, both local and national. Parallel to this development, other sectors of the culture and media industry (such as advertisement, music, and the press) have also undergone a rapid growth process. Interestingly, these developments first had a negative impact on Turkish cinema (Dorsay, 2004). For the audience of the 1990s, who could watch television shows for free and the latest Hollywood productions in luxurious movie theaters, the amateurish, low-quality domestic productions shown in second-rank movie theaters were no longer attractive. Meanwhile, the audience profile of Turkish cinema had also changed. With the improving standards of movie theaters, ticket prices increased. Cinema is no longer a lower-middle class entertainment, and families no longer constitute its primary audience. The new moviegoers are educated, young, middle- and upper-middle-class urbanites (Maktav, 2001/2).

The 1990s were an ambivalent decade for Turkey, leading to bleak events in society along with some promising developments. Throughout most of these years, Turkey experienced a protracted conflict between separatist Kurdish guerillas and the Turkish army, claiming an estimated 30,000 lives, mostly persons of Kurdish origin.[8] In the mid-1990s, more than 1,500 rural settlements were evacuated as part of the military campaign against guerilla forces, leading to the massive displacement of Kurdish peasants (Keyder, 2004). In 1999, after the arrest of Abdullah Öcalan, the leader of the PKK (Kurdistan Workers' Party), the ethnicized violence decreased and a new process of democratization began. As the discord in eastern Turkey temporarily came to an end, Turkey's relations with the European Union (EU) improved, and at the 1999 Helsinki EU Summit, Turkey's candidacy for EU membership was for the first time officially announced. Despite the anti-Turkish sentiments prevailing in several EU countries, full membership negotiations between Turkey and the EU officially began in October 2005. A reform process started after the EU's declaration of Turkish candidacy for membership and gathered speed with the 2002 election of the Justice and Development Party (AKP), which received 37 percent of the vote. Regardless of its Islamic background, the AKP government played a key role in the reform and democratization process (Keyder, 2004). Civil society movements supported the AKP government's efforts in the candidacy process since they saw it as the only way of achieving greater democracy, rule of law, and an expanded pluralism. By the end of the 1990s, the moderate wings of Islamic and Kurdish movements had joined the ranks of civil society and human rights activists advocating rapid fulfillment of the conditions required by Brussels (Keyder, 2004).

The advancement of the EU process has also given rise to the proliferation of nationalist discourses in Turkey. Parallel to the global nationalist trend, visible particularly in the triangle formed by the Balkans, the Middle East, and the Caucasus, Turkish nationalism gained momentum in the late 1980s and 1990s (Bora, 2003). Perceiving the EU process as a threat to the unity and sovereignty of the country, nationalist discourses spread aggressively in the 2000s, to encompass not only the entire political right, but also several branches of the left. In the meantime, security in eastern and southeastern Turkey deteriorated again, and clashes between the armed forces and Kurdish guerillas were renewed. As the number of military casualties increased, nationalist movements gained further strength. By 2007, the reform process had come to a halt, already having slowed down over the course of 2006. This was due to various European countries' increasing opposition to Turkey's EU membership, which weakened the position of the reformist AKP government. It was also the result of the AKP's declining commitment to the reform process, in the interest of attracting nationalist votes for the 2007 parliamentary elections in which it was re-elected by gaining nearly 50 percent of the votes (Kurban, 2007).

The recent transformation of Turkish society is based on a struggle between various forces, interests, and voices. This has been a period of ethnic and nationalist violence, as well as of great efforts towards peace, democratization, and pluralism. Ayşe Gül Altınay describes this difficult process as follows:

> The military intervention of 1980, the re-writing of the constitution by the military regime in 1982, and the internal war between the PKK

(Kurdistan Workers' Party) and the state security forces in the 1990s significantly militarized Turkish political discourse and practice. Characterized by polarization, antagonism, 'win or lose' logic, the normalization of violence, and ethnic nationalisms (both Turkish and Kurdish), this militarized political space left little room for voices of democratization and pluralism to articulate themselves. Still, the same period witnessed a proliferation of political organizing against militarization, nationalism and discrimination of all sorts. Feminist movements, human rights activism, gay and lesbian organizations, conscientious objectors, nonviolence training groups, and peace initiatives challenged the existing political discourse and proposed a new language to approach difference in the context of a democratic polity. (Altınay: 2007: 22)

It was in the context of these complex developments that new wave Turkish cinema was born.[9] After a period of grave recession and crisis, the mid-1990s witnessed a remarkable revival of Turkish cinema in two separate forms: a new popular cinema with considerable box-office success on the one hand, and an art cinema receiving critical acclaim and prestigious awards in national and international festivals on the other. The motivational force behind both modes of film production was a new generation of young directors who made their first feature films after the mid-1990s.

Turkish film critics generally consider Yavuz Turgul's 1996 film *The Bandit* (*Eşkıya*) to have inaugurated new popular Turkish cinema. *The Bandit* merges classical Yeşilçam themes with flawless visuals in the grand style of Hollywood productions. It addresses issues that Yeşilçam cinema had again and again raised in the past, such as the decision to choose 'money versus love, love versus paternal responsibility, dedication versus individual freedom, all boiling down to redemption and sacrifice' (Erdoğan, 2002: 234). It is, however, a 'post-Yeşilçam film' in the sense that its cinematography, soundtrack, special effects, and editing display a technical perfection comparable to that of Hollywood productions (Erdoğan and Göktürk, 2001: 549).

With *The Bandit*, Turkish cinema reversed its fortunes in terms of box-office success. Reaching a record number of more than 2.5 million viewers in the movie theaters, *The Bandit* succeeded in making Turkish films attractive again.[10] Compared to the extremely low viewer numbers of the previous decade, an audience of 2.5 million for one single film was a miraculous achievement. Furthermore, *The Bandit* owes its success not to a successful advertising campaign – in fact, very little money was spent on promotion – but to the viewers' appreciation. Unlike films promoted by elaborate campaigns, *The Bandit* attracted the largest audience not in the first week of its release, but in the fourth one. Evidently, viewers spread favorable opinions about the film by word of mouth, and the size of the audience gradually increased.

The Bandit became not only a major blockbuster, but also a model for later box-office success. Following the same formula, many popular Turkish films of the late 1990s and early 2000s combined technical features of contemporary Hollywood blockbusters – such as fast editing, mobile camera, fast action, and flawless *mise-en-scène* – with an ironic handling of Yeşilçam themes. The commercial success of popular cinema gradually grew in the years following the production of *The Bandit*. Eventually, box-office rates of above 1 million viewers became common for popular Turkish films.

The new popular cinema has generated its financial resources not so much from the film business, but from other segments of the culture and media industry, most notably television and advertising. As successful professionals in television and/ or advertising, the star directors of popular cinema – among them Çağan Irmak, Ezel Akay, Mustafa Altıoklar, Osman Sınav, Ömer Faruk Sorak, Serdar Akar, Sinan Çetin, Yavuz Turgul, and Yılmaz Erdoğan – finance their big-budget films mostly with the help of the revenues and business contacts generated from these sectors.[11] Receiving widespread promotion and distribution on the domestic market, their films have not only earned considerable box-office revenues in Turkey, but they are also distributed in European cities that have a large population of Turkish migrants.

In 2001, Yılmaz Erdoğan's directoral debut *Vizontele* (co-directed by Ömer Faruk Sorak) surpassed the record of *The Bandit* and reached more than 3.3 million viewers.[12] Already a popular television star, Erdoğan as the leading actor and director was presumably a primary factor in attracting viewers. Telling the story of the introduction of television to a remote town in eastern Turkey during the 1970s, *Vizontele* reproduces to some extent Yılmaz Erdoğan's already familiar comedy style.

In 2004, *G.O.R.A.*, a film starring the popular stand-up comedian Cem Yılmaz, became the new record-breaking blockbuster with more than 4 million viewers.[13] A parody of space-odyssey films, *G.O.R.A.* depicts what would happen if a 'Turk' were abducted by aliens and found himself on a spaceship. Although directed by Ömer Faruk Sorak, the co-director of *Vizontele*, the film is often credited to Cem Yılmaz, who wrote the story and played the two main characters, the hero and the villain. The following year, a melodrama blended with humor, *My Father and My Son* (*Babam ve Oğlum*), became a blockbuster, reaching an audience of more than 3.8 million.[14] Telling the story of a difficult relationship between a father and a son in an Aegean town in the aftermath of the 12 September 1980 coup, *My Father and My Son* is directed by Çağan Irmak, the renowned director of a popular television drama series. As a result of the commercial vitality created by these and many other popular films, Turkish cinema reconquered the domestic market. In 2006, Serdar Akar's American-style, yet anti-American action adventure film *Valley of the Wolves Iraq* (*Kurtlar Vadisi Irak*) set a new record, reaching more than 4.2 million viewers in Turkey.[15] Based on a Turkish hit television series, this was the most expensive Turkish film ever made, with a budget exceeding US$10 million; *Valley of the Wolves Iraq* also attracted a record number of viewers abroad: more than 500,000.[16]

In 1996, the year when *The Bandit* succeeded at the box office, Derviş Zaim's *Somersault in the Coffin* (*Tabutta Rövaşata*) was also released. *Somersault in the Coffin* was not a success in commercial terms, yet, with its unconventional story and innovative cinematic style, many consider it as the film that inaugurated new wave art cinema. Zaim's debut work as director and screenwriter, *Somersault in the Coffin* gives an account of life in Istanbul from the perspective of a homeless man. The film was made on a minuscule budget and under quite amateurish conditions. In the subsequent years, films such as *The Small Town* (*Kasaba*, Nuri Bilge Ceylan, 1997), *Innocence* (*Masumiyet*, Zeki Demirkubuz, 1997), and *Journey to the Sun* (*Güneşe Yolculuk*, Yeşim Ustaoğlu, 1999) followed a similar path. They all have a distinct cinematic style unique in the history of Turkish cinema. Despite the critical acclaim that these films earned at international festivals, they attracted only a relatively small audience in Turkey and did not receive much media attention. It was not until several films received considerable international acclaim in the 2000s that new wave art cinema was recognized at home. In 2002, two films by Zeki Demirkubuz, *Fate* (*Yazgı*, 2001) and *Confession* (*İtiraf*, 2001), were invited to be shown under the prestigious division of *un certain regard* at the Cannes Film Festival. The following year, Nuri Bilge Ceylan's *Distant* (*Uzak*, 2002) won both the Grand Jury Prize and acting awards for its two male lead characters (Mehmet Emin Toprak and Muzaffer Özdemir) at the same festival.[17] In 2004, *Head-On* (*Gegen Die Wand/Duvara Karşı*), not a Turkish film per se, but a film by the Turkish-German director Fatih Akın, won the European Film Award and the Golden Bear at the Berlin Film Festival. In 2006, Nuri Bilge Ceylan's next film, *Climates* (*İklimler*, 2006), received the Fipresci Prize at the Cannes Film Festival.[18] These and other awards have brought visibility to new wave art cinema both in Turkey and abroad.

Ahmet Uluçay, Derviş Zaim, Handan İpekçi, Kutluğ Ataman, Nuri Bilge Ceylan, Reha Erdem, Semih Kaplanoğlu,

Tayfun Pirselimoğlu, Uğur Yücel, Yeşim Ustaoğlu, and Zeki Demirkubuz are among the most prominent directors of the new art cinema.

II

This book examines the development of new wave Turkish cinema in relation to notions of 'belonging,' 'identity,' and 'memory' against the backdrop of Turkish society's recent transformation. I argue that new wave Turkish cinema, popular and art films alike, constantly returns to the question of belonging and interrogates it from different social, political, and aesthetic perspectives. New Turkish films revolve around the figure of a 'spectral home,' which takes different forms and meanings in the work of different directors.

Nostalgic remembrance of the past is a recurrent theme one often encounters in the new popular cinema. Chapter 1 discusses new popular films that focus on the provincial small-town life of the past, under the category of 'popular nostalgia cinema.' Among the films discussed in this chapter are *Propaganda* (Sinan Çetin, 1999), *Offside* (*Dar Alanda Kısa Paslaşmalar*, Serdar Akar, 2000), *The Waterfall* (*Şellale*, Semir Aslanyürek, 2001), *Vizontele* (Yılmaz Erdoğan, 2001), *Vizontele Tuuba* (Yılmaz Erdoğan, 2004), *My Father and My Son* (*Babam ve Oğlum*, Çağan Irmak, 2005), and *The International* (*Beynelmilel*, Sırrı Süreyya Önder and Muharrem Gülmez, 2006). Drawing upon Gaston Bachelard's (1994 [first published 1958]) conception of the childhood home as an image of 'felicitous space,' I argue that Turkish nostalgia films are imaginary accounts of the past as a period of collective childhood – that is, as a period of the childhood of society as a whole. The spectral home at the center of the new popular cinema, in this sense, is haunted by a nostalgic yearning for a long-lost childhood. Nostalgia films voice a critique of present-day Turkey through an idealized representation of the past as an age of collective childhood. This critique, however, is problematic in the sense that it renders society unaccountable for the events of the past and saves it from the burden of responsibility. In popular nostalgia films, while malice is externalized because it is associated with the intervention of outside forces (often in the form of the authoritarian state, military intervention, or neo-liberal economic policies), the presumed innocence and integrity of home is left intact. Rather than engaging in a critical interrogation of the past, Turkish nostalgia films arrest the past in an image of frozen childhood. Adopting the distinction that Svetlana Boym (2001) makes between the 'reflective' and 'restorative' modes of nostalgia, I contend that Turkish nostalgia films are accounts of reflective nostalgia. In fact, nostalgia films become most interesting in those moments when they reflect upon the ambivalences of longing and belonging. Those ambivalent moments are often found in the marginal details and secondary themes of the story. Although new popular films mostly invoke a reflective mode, restorative nostalgia is not altogether absent from contemporary Turkish cinema. *Valley of the Wolves Iraq* can actually be seen as a prominent manifestation of restorative nostalgia. Pointing to the continuity between the reflective and restorative modes of nostalgia, this chapter finally attempts to establish that popular nostalgia films promote a romantic and celebratory vision of belonging, which precludes a critical engagement with the past.

Chapter 2 is devoted to the discussion of new wave political cinema. Drawing upon films such as *Journey to the Sun* (*Güneşe Yolculuk*, Yeşim Ustaoğlu, 1999), *In Nowhere Land* (*Hiçbiryerde*, Tayfun Pirselimoğlu, 2002), *Mud* (*Çamur*, Derviş Zaim, 2003), *Waiting for the Clouds* (*Bulutları Beklerken*, Yeşim Ustaoğlu, 2003), and *Toss Up* (*Yazı/Tura*, Uğur Yücel, 2004), this chapter attempts to show how new wave political cinema critically faces the past. The past that one encounters here is not nostalgic, but traumatic. The spectral home at the center of these films is haunted by the traumatic events of the past. Discussing issues such as the conflict between the Turkish army and the separatist Kurdish guerillas in the southeast, police brutality against political prisoners, people who disappear while under police custody, discriminatory policies against religious and ethnic minorities, and so forth, new political films typically focus attention on how the lives of ordinary people have been destroyed by Turkey's turbulent political climate of the recent past. Unlike popular nostalgia films, which avoid serious engagement with past political events other than in the form of a light-hearted critique within the conventions of dark comedy, new political films focus attention directly on the question of how to come to terms with a traumatic past. This chapter argues that Turkey's new wave political cinema has in fact much in common with the emerging independent transnational cinema in its relentless interrogation of questions of national belonging and identity.

In the context of new wave Turkish cinema, two names particularly stand out as prominent *auteur*-directors of their generation, because of the peculiarity of their *oeuvre* and the international acclaim that their films receive: Nuri Bilge Ceylan and Zeki Demirkubuz. Although neither of these directors directly engages in political issues, their films are implicitly political in their relentless interrogation of the question of belonging. In contrast to the popular nostalgia films that describe situations in which home is threatened from outside, the films by Ceylan and Demirkubuz focus on situations where home is challenged from within. 'We can always defend ourselves or even rebuild after the home has been attacked from outside,' writes Nikos Papastergiadis (1998: 3), 'but how do you deal with that slow but determined process of implosion?' It is this very process of the home's implosion that the cinema of Ceylan and Demirkubuz describes.

Nuri Bilge Ceylan is arguably the most internationally acclaimed director of the new Turkish cinema, especially after he received the Grand Jury Price for *Distant* at Cannes in 2003. The films that Ceylan has made so far – *Cocoon* (*Koza*, 1995), *The Small Town* (*Kasaba*, 1997), *Clouds of May* (*Mayıs Sıkıntısı*,

18

1999), *Distant* (*Uzak*, 2002), and *Climates* (*İklimler*, 2006) – are characterized by a thematic and visual unity. The tropes of home and belonging constitute his central thematic preoccupation. Belonging is often discussed in relation to the question of provinciality. The province signifies not a particular locality, but a mode of feeling: ennui resulting from being stuck in a limiting place where one supposedly belongs. In this sense, provinciality might embrace the small town as well as the big city. The images that Ceylan employs in exploring the themes of home and belonging recall Gilles Deleuze's (1989) vision of the 'time-image' cinema. Drawing upon Deleuze's concept, Chapter 3 attempts to reveal the paradoxical structure of home in Ceylan's cinema. Home, in his films, connotes both confinement and comfort, entrapment and ease. A certain notion of play is also intrinsic to Ceylan's cinema. Playing is articulated in his films on three levels: in relation to children and their play; in relation to adults and their everyday activities; and in relation to the process of filmmaking itself. Utilizing Donald W. Winnicott's (1982) understanding of playing as an experience that helps acknowledge a paradox without necessarily seeking to resolve it, Chapter 3 suggests that Ceylan's cinema is, more than anything, about acknowledging the paradoxes of home and belonging.

Zeki Demirkubuz is another *auteur*-director of the new Turkish cinema. To date he has made seven feature films, which have a thematic and visual unity. Demirkubuz' films have closely plotted structures, and tend to center on characters who are either agitated or detached. In contrast to the ordinary situations of everyday life depicted by Ceylan, Demirkubuz' films always draw upon highly dramatic and violent events, often murder and/or suicide. Chapter 4 discusses how Demirkubuz' films direct attention to the dark underside of domesticity and home. In Demirkubuz' cinema, home appears to be haunted by routine malice. The houses we see in his films are always depicted as claustrophobic places. Stripped of all of its romantic connotations, home is represented as a place of confinement, a prison that enslaves its inhabitants. Thus, the prevailing mood in Demirkubuz' cinema is that of claustrophobia. This mood is visually conveyed in the *mise-en-scène* through the excessive use of claustrophobic interiors. Events usually take place in gloomy apartments or hotel rooms that look very much alike. The sense of compulsive repetition is another peculiar characteristic of Demirkubuz' cinema; this deepens the claustrophobic and dark tone of his films. In a confined world, everything perpetually duplicates itself. Again and again, similar situations occur between different characters. The sense of compulsive repetition in the narrative leads to an abyssal structure that produces an uncanny feeling.

One interesting aspect of new Turkish cinema is Istanbul's fading out of the screen. New wave Turkish films concentrate not so much on Istanbul, but on provincial towns. In those instances when the story is set in Istanbul, the geographical, historical, and cultural characteristics of the city are often erased so that Istanbul turns into an oversized provincial town. In contrast to the privileged position of Istanbul in Turkish film history, the majority of the new wave films seem to have lost interest in the city. However, this does not mean that Istanbul has disappeared from contemporary films altogether. Instead, we can talk about the emergence of a new transnational genre of 'Istanbul films' that offer alternative ways of seeing the city. Chapter 5 examines different strategies of representing Istanbul in four films of the last decade, offering new modalities of thinking about the city's recent transformation. *Somersault in the Coffin* can be considered a pioneering example of the new Istanbul films, giving view of the city through the eyes of a homeless man who lives on the Bosphorus. In contrast to the realism of *Somersault in the Coffin, Istanbul Tales (Anlat Istanbul*, 2005), a film directed by five different directors (Ümit Ünal, Kudret Sabancı, Selim Demirdelen, Yücel Yolcu, and Ömür Atay), reflects a flamboyant image of the city. Telling five different yet overlapping stories about the intersecting lives of characters from different backgrounds, *Istanbul Tales* adapts well-known fairytales to modern-day Istanbul. Finally, Fatih Akın's *Head-On* (*Duvara Karşı/Gegen die Wand*, 2004) and *Crossing the Bridge: The Sound of Istanbul* (*Istanbul Hatırası*, 2005) reflect a peculiar image of the city. *Head-On* is a love story that takes place in two cities, Hamburg and Istanbul, whereas *Crossing the Bridge* is a documentary on the diverse music scene of Istanbul. Challenging the notion of an authentic cultural identity, both films represent Istanbul as a city in constant motion, a chaotic fusion of influences, interactions, and traditions. Of course, as German productions, neither *Head-On* nor *Crossing the Bridge* is part of new Turkish cinema. Yet, the peculiar imagery of Istanbul that these films employ enables us to classify them as transnational Istanbul films by a Turkish-German director. New Istanbul films, Chapter 5 maintains, tackle clichés about Istanbul. Instead of negating them, they rather recycle clichés to make new uses of them.

Chapter 6 seeks to engage in an overall discussion of the new Turkish cinema and gender. Interestingly, the absence of women is one of the defining characteristics of new wave cinema. In a great majority of new wave films, the story revolves around male characters; women are portrayed not as active subjects, but as objects of male desire. This absence, however, should not necessarily be considered an altogether negative condition in relation to the gender politics of new Turkish cinema. The position of new wave films towards women, Chapter 6 suggests, is shaped around a certain ambivalence. These films, on the one hand, subordinate women to men and deny them agency. This male-dominant attitude is of course problematic, for it reproduces the still powerful patriarchal culture in Turkish society. On the other hand, however, we can also detect a positive element in this masculinist picture, in the sense that new wave films sometimes exhibit a critical self-awareness about their own complicity with patriarchal culture. This chapter examines the ambivalent gender politics of new Turkish cinema through a discussion of *Vasfiye Is Her Name* (*Adı Vasfiye*), a 1985 film by veteran director Atıf Yılmaz, made a decade prior to the emergence of the new wave.[19] In addition to its innovative cinematic style, Yılmaz's film is important in Turkish film history because of its subversive gender politics. Chapter 6 discusses *Vasfiye Is Her Name* as a paradigmatic text to make sense of the gender politics of new wave cinema.

Chapter 7, the afterword, aims to provide a general assessment of new wave Turkish cinema on the basis of the arguments of the preceding chapters.

III

An earlier and quite different version of this book was published by Metis Press, Istanbul, in the spring of 2006. The present volume is more of a reminiscence of the original volume than its repetition, for it includes extensive revisions. Some parts have been substantially revised, while others have been written anew. The original volume has been updated to include several significant works released after its publication. It has also been revised for readers who are not necessarily familiar with Turkey's recent history.

I would like to conclude here by pointing to some short-comings of this book. It is always a challenge to write on an evolving cultural phenomenon. Hence, I know that my efforts to update the content of the book will ultimately remain futile in the face of the continuing developments of Turkish cinema. Also, the specific conceptual framework that one employs to make cultural developments intelligible will inevitably impose artificial boundaries on cultural phenomena and result in fore-grounding certain works while downplaying others. The distinction that I make between the categories of 'popular' and 'art' cinema is certainly an artificial one, and its explanatory power is limited, given the actual divergence of films. Similarly, I cannot claim that I have done justice to all the films of new Turkish cinema. Significant works might have been left out or insufficiently covered, either because they cannot be easily related to the book's conceptual framework, or because they were released only after its completion. However, these shortcomings also point to possible areas for future research on new Turkish cinema.

1

POPULAR NOSTALGIA FILMS

If the new Turkish cinema revolves around the figure of a 'spectral home,' in popular films this home is haunted by a nostalgic yearning for a long-lost childhood. The spectral home at the center of the new popular cinema is imagined as a locus of untainted innocence, harmony, and cordial relationships.

Nostalgic remembrance of the past is a theme one often encounters in the new popular cinema. We can even suggest that recent popular films focusing on the past constitute a sub-genre in themselves, on the basis of their striking thematic and visual resemblance. In terms of their thematic preoccupations, these films typically focus on provincial small-town life of the recent past. For example, *Propaganda* (Sinan Çetin, 1999), a film ridiculing oppressive and irrational state authority, is set in an unidentified provincial town in eastern Turkey in 1948. *Offside* (*Dar Alanda Kısa Paslaşmalar*, Serdar Akar, 2000) recounts the story of an amateur soccer team in 1982 in Bursa, a small city in northwestern Turkey. *The Waterfall* (*Şellale*, Semir Aslanyürek, 2001) is set in 1960 Antakya, a town on the Syrian border of Turkey. It describes the period shortly before the military intervention on 27 May 1960. Yılmaz Erdoğan's 2001 film *Vizontele* is set in Van, a town in eastern Turkey, in 1974. It is about the townspeople's initiation into the world of television.

Vizontele Tuuba (Yılmaz Erdoğan, 2004), the sequel to *Vizontele*, is set in the same town and describes the events taking place shortly before the military coup on 12 September 1980. Set in a small town on the Aegean coast during the aftermath of the same coup, *My Father and My Son* (*Babam ve Oğlum*, Çağan Irmak, 2005) is about the difficult relationship between a traditional father and his rebellious son. Also focusing on the 12 September 1980 military intervention, *The International* (*Beynelmilel*, Sırrı Süreyya Önder and Muharrem Gülmez, 2006) tells the tragicomic story of a local band formed on order of the martial law commanders in Adıyaman, a town in southeastern Anatolia.[1]

Although these films are all about the past, and often about past political events, it would be misleading to call them 'historical films,' since they do not intend to produce an objective account of the past.[2] Instead, they emphasize subjective accounts of memory shaped around a strong sense of nostalgia. I will discuss these films under the category of 'nostalgia cinema.'[3]

I

Turkish nostalgia films put emphasis not so much on the past, but on the remembrance of the past from today's perspective. In other words, these films foreground a subjective account of memory and yearning for a lost past. The past remembered in nostalgia films has an intimate quality, akin to childhood memories. Their atmosphere is somewhat reminiscent of what Gaston Bachelard (1994: xxxvi) calls 'images of felicitous space.' Bachelard has a particularly spatialized conception of memory. For him, lived time as opposed to abstract time is defined by its spatial specificity, its localization. Space gives quality to time. In this context, Bachelard defines 'felicitous space' as a space that is 'lived in, not in its positivity, but with all the partiality of the imagination' (1994: xxxvi). The privileged image of felicitous space is that of the 'house.' 'For our house,' he writes, 'is our corner of the world. As has often been said, it is our first universe, a real cosmos in every sense of the word' (Bachelard, 1994: 4). However our childhood might have been, when we daydream about it, we produce an image of protection, intimacy, and well-being. The protective value of the house of our childhood makes it the utmost felicitous space. 'Life begins well, it begins enclosed, protected, all warm in the bosom of the house [. . .] When we dream of the house we were born in, in the utmost depths of reverie, we participate in this original warmth, in this well-tempered matter of the material paradise' (Bachelard, 1994: 7). In Bachelard's conceptualization, memory and imagination remain associated with the realm of 'felicitous space.' The past endures in the imagination, not in the facts: 'It is on the plane of the daydream and not on that of facts that childhood remains alive [. . .] Through this permanent childhood, we maintain the poetry of the past' (Bachelard, 1994: 16). Childhood, then, is something that we never leave behind; on the contrary, we need to grow old to experience our youth. This is youth transformed by imagination and memory, and it is something greater than the reality of childhood.

In Turkish nostalgia films, I suggest, the provincial small-town setting of the recent past is transformed into an image of the felicitous space of childhood. These films attribute a protective and hospitable value to the provincial town-life of the past. The enclosed world of the provincial town is comparable to the protective and embracing aspects of the childhood house. In this sense, Turkish nostalgia films are accounts of imagining the past as a period of collective childhood – that is, a period of the childhood of society as a whole. In these films, the provincial town-life of the past is transformed into an image of the felicitous space of childhood.

Having said this, however, I should also acknowledge that Turkish nostalgia films have an ambivalent relationship to the condition of 'provinciality' that they describe. It is possible to talk about a double articulation of the 'province' in these films: as a space of both melancholy and joy. On the one hand, the province appears in these films as a site of limitations, backwardness, and destitution. The dominant structure of feeling in each film is that of a subtle melancholy arising from the peculiar experience of provinciality. In one scene in *Vizontele*, for example, the mayor describes his town as the 'capital of disappointment.' The province connotes remoteness and having been left behind.

On the other hand, in nostalgia films the province is also depicted as a site of uncontaminated cordial relationships and happiness. Far from being depressing, the provincial small-town atmosphere of the recent past is constructed as very joyful. The marked aesthetization of visual elements contributes to the peculiar ambience of the films. Instead of reducing the province to a cultural void, each film gives it a distinctive face. Each film deliberately emphasizes the natural and historical assets of the town that it depicts. *The Waterfall*, for example, underscores the long history of the city of Antakya. In *Offside*, the distinctive architecture of the old city of Bursa is accentuated. *Vizontele* and *Vizontele Tuuba* offer noticeably aestheticized landscape shots displaying the stunning scenery of eastern Anatolia. While the province is reinvented in nostalgia films as a secret world with hidden treasures, the provincial town-life of the past is turned into a lost paradise. In this sense, confinement to a small community functions not only as a limitation, but also as a form of protection against the outside world. The small-town community with its intimate and cordial relationships is like an extended family. Everybody in the community knows each other. Even the harshest conflicts seem naive and innocent. In this way, nostalgia films evoke an imaginary condition of feeling perfectly at home in the place where one belongs. The relationship of the subject to his/her homeland is envisioned as that of complete harmony, unity, and inclusion. Like Bachelard's description of the house of our childhood, the provincial town is depicted in these films as the characters' corner of the world.

In popular nostalgia films, then, the provincial small-town environment of the recent past functions as a protective shell, akin to the image of the house in childhood memories. The sense of harmony and innocence prevailing in these films, however, involves also a certain vulnerability. The blissful atmosphere of the stories appears too good to be true. Hence, there emerges the anticipation of an approaching menace. In nostalgia films, the narrative comprises a dichotomous structure based on inside/outside and before/after. The unfolding of the story in each film creates the impression that the events we see occur during a period *before* something damaging happens, as if located prior to the interruption of a devastating outside force. In this sense, the temporal structure of nostalgia films articulates a sense of 'once upon a time.' They seem to describe an idealized world that existed before the loss of social harmony and innocence. While something inherently good is attributed to the small-community life of the past, it is contrasted with the menace of the subsequent period. In each film, the story points to a moment when the protective shell of the childhood home/ hometown is irrecoverably destroyed by an outside force.

In Turkish nostalgia films, the outside force that disrupts the internal harmony of home is often connected to the idea of the central government's intervention in local community matters. The form of this intervention might vary, but in all cases the film engages in a subtle critique of state authority in Turkey. This critique has to do with the peculiarity of the way in which the concept of the state is perceived in Turkish society. The state, in Çağlar Keyder's words, is a concept with an unequivocal referent in the Turkish context: 'In its eyes, the nation is an organic totality whose true interests can be known and fostered only by the Kemalist governing elite. It calls for constant vigilance against the forces who would dismantle the country and threaten Turkish national unity' (2004: 65). In this defensive understanding of the state, the Turkish armed forces perceive themselves as privileged. As a consequence of their character as the 'state-founding military,' identified with Mustafa Kemal, the founding figure of the Republic, the army considers itself to be the 'true owner' and 'personified symbol' of the country (Bora, 2003: 437). This explains why in the history of modern Turkey the military disrupted the democratic order three times – on 27 May 1960, 12 March 1971, and 12 September 1980 – under the pretext of protecting the country against 'internal and external enemies' that threatened its unity. The periods of martial law have left deep scars on Turkish democracy.

Among the popular nostalgia films discussed in this chapter, *Propaganda* probably engages most directly in a critique of excessive state authority in Turkey. The interrupting outside force in *Propaganda* is represented by a customs officer appointed to a small border town in eastern Turkey in 1948. The first act of the new officer is to give orders to construct a barbed-wire fence along the border. At first, the townspeople do not fully comprehend the consequences of this development and celebrate it as a novelty that adds interest to their lives. They happily comply with the procedure at the checkpoints, as though they were playing a game. Once the construction of the barbed-wire fence is completed, however, they begin to realize the nature of the problem. On the basis of the meticulous measurements conducted by the customs officer and his deputy, the border fence is constructed in such a way that it divides the town in two. People can no longer pass from one side to the other without a passport. As a result, families are divided, lovers separated. The border brings nothing but misery to the town.

The narrative of *Propaganda* clearly comprises a dichotomous structure based on inside/outside and before/after. The blissful atmosphere of small-community life is interrupted by the arrival of the customs officer appointed from Ankara, the capital where the central government is located. The film draws upon a stark distinction between the local community and the state-appointed officers to make the difference between inside and outside clear. While the townspeople are depicted as happy and friendly, the officers are always rude. In contrast to the colorful ethnic costume of the townspeople, the officers wear dark uniforms.

Unlike the townspeople, whose lively language is colored by different ethnic accents and idioms, the officers speak only the limited vocabulary of the official discourse. The barbed wire dividing the town in two functions as a symbol of the central government's intervention in local community life. Although the borderline serves no meaningful purpose, the customs officer and his deputy remain adamant about following the orders to set up the fence in this location. The more the townspeople revolt against the new policy, the more rigid the officers become. In their mind, taking a step back would mean undermining state authority. Not seeing itself as being in the service of society, the state in Turkey remains a self-serving power preoccupied with the idea of expanding its authority. Thus, state elites take irrational and excessive measures in situations that they perceive as eroding the privileged status of the state. Demonstrating the destructive consequences of the state's intervention in civil life, *Propaganda* critiques unwarranted state authority in Turkey.[4]

While the criticism against the interventionist state in *Propaganda* is quite straightforward, Yılmaz Erdoğan's blockbuster, *Vizontele*, engages in a more subtle critique. Set in 1974 in eastern Turkey, the outside force disrupting local community life in this film consists of the first television broadcasting. At the beginning of the film, the mayor hears a rumor about the imminent arrival of television broadcasting in their town. At this point, no one in town has the slightest idea of the meaning of the word 'television.' One day, civil servants from Ankara arrive in town to transport some technical equipment, then leave immediately without explaining how to install it. After this point, the story revolves around the mayor's attempts to set up the transmitter with the help of a former student of his. After much trial and error and discouraging failures, they finally succeed in receiving the television broadcast. This becomes a cause for celebration in town. Groups of people pour into the mayor's house to see television broadcasting for the first time in their lives. Tragically, however, this becomes a night of mourning rather than celebration when they see on prime-time news that the mayor's youngest son, who had joined the army for his compulsory military service, was killed during the conflict in Cyprus in 1974.

In the same way in which the construction of a border fence is at first perceived in positive terms in *Propaganda*, television in *Vizontele* is initially seen by the townspeople as a medium that will connect their remote town to the center. Through the television programs of the state-controlled TRT, they expect to gain direct access to developments in the center. However, soon they realize that being closer to the center is not necessarily to their advantage. The killing of the mayor's son in Cyprus functions as an allegorical reference to the wave of devastation that would plunge all of eastern Anatolia into a war between the Turkish army and the separatist Kurdish guerillas in the years to come.

Narrating the story of an amateur soccer team in Bursa in 1982, the outside force disrupting community life in *Offside* is a capitalist-minded young entrepreneur who represents the rising neo-liberal values of the 1980s. The film revolves around the relations between the amateur football players, their coach, and the local tradesmen who sponsor the team. Although adults, the characters are quite child-like in their sincere and whole-hearted commitment to the survival of their team. This picture of happiness, however, is disrupted when a young entrepreneur comes to town to purchase the team against the will of the players. In the end, the devoted coach who acts as a father figure to his players dies of cancer. No longer receiving sufficient support from the local tradesmen because of financial difficulties, the team in the end is sold to the young entrepreneur. This marks the end of harmonious community life in the story.

Apart from the oppressive political regime that came to power after the military coup on 12 September 1980, the 1980s also saw the introduction of a series of neo-liberal reforms that paved the way for increasing deregulation and privatization of the economic system. As a result of the implementation of these economic reforms, corruption became a widespread reality of everyday life. A class of *nouveau riche* emerged during this era, making a fortune from the irregularities of the new economic system. The young entrepreneur in *Offside* is a representative of this class. His interest in the local soccer team is actually part of a larger plan of starting a professional – hence more profitable – team. Considering only his own self-interest, he embraces the values of individualism, materialism, and competitiveness. The end of the harmonious small-town life in *Offside*, then, is brought about by the intervention of the rising neo-liberal values of the 1980s.

In *The Waterfall*, *Vizontele Tuuba*, *My Father and My Son*, and *The International*, the outside force that shatters the protective shell of small-town life is military intervention. While *The Waterfall* focuses on the coup of 27 May 1960, the other three films deal with the 12 September 1980 intervention. All four films are critical of military intervention.

The Waterfall depicts the events, shortly before the 27 May incident, in Antakya, a southern Anatolian town, from the perspective of a man who visits his native town and remembers the events of his childhood. The story focuses on two brothers (one of them is the father of the protagonist) who live with their families in the same house, without speaking to each other. The dispute that divides the brothers and their family home is a political one. While the father of the protagonist is a devoted member of the right-wing Democratic Party, his brother supports the statist Republican People's Party. In fact, not just this household, but the entire town is polarized between the two parties. This is not a serious disagreement about political ideas, but rather a juvenile and highly personalized discord. Discussions on political matters among the townspeople are extremely simplistic and always end up in cursing and fistfights. The film underlines the naive and innocent tone of the relationships in the local community. This childish political friction in the town gradually culminates until, in the end, the father of the protagonist is arrested for supporting a strike. Afraid that the police might search their house, his wife wants to destroy any potentially 'illegal' materials such as alcoholic beverages and books. As she tries to set the books on fire, her little daughter is wounded and later dies in the hospital. The following morning, martial law is declared. The death of the small daughter in *The Waterfall*, just like the death of the young son in *Vizontele*, becomes a symbol for the devastation that the central government's intervention might bring to the lives of ordinary people. In each case, the loss of a child represents the end of innocent and happy times for the community.

Vizontele Tuuba, the sequel to *Vizontele*, recounts the period shortly before the 12 September 1980 coup. Like *The Waterfall*, it offers an account of the military intervention as a childhood memory. Set in the same town as *Vizontele*, and using voice-over, the film narrates the events of the summer of 1980 in the town, from the point of view of its main character, Yılmaz (Şenol Ballı) (the namesake of the director), who was an adolescent back then. We hear the director's own voice as the invisible narrator of the film; the autobiographical elements in the film suggest that the story is a personal account of the director's own childhood. The film opens in a high-school classroom in October 1980, where Yılmaz struggles to carry out a writing assignment about how he spent the summer. 'It was a difficult question,' the voice-over says, 'it was very difficult for everyone who used to be a child back then. I think that was the last summer of my childhood.' Not managing to complete the assignment, Yılmaz writes only a single word on the paper: 'TUUBA.' Then the narrative moves back in time to June of 1980, showing Yılmaz on a bus traveling from Istanbul to Van, his hometown, to spend the summer holiday with his family. Tuuba is the name of a young girl whom he meets (and instantly falls in love with) on the bus, the disabled daughter of a librarian who is exiled to eastern Turkey. Unlike the customs officer in *Propaganda*, the librarian in *Vizontele Tuuba* is not a representative of state authority, since he himself has been punished by the state for his dissident ideas. The story shows the librarian's efforts to establish a public library in town. Despite the initial indifference of the local people, his hard work gradually pays off, and in the end, he succeeds not only in converting an abandoned building into a small, charming library, but also in attracting the townspeople to it. All these accomplishments, however, end in oblivion on the morning of 12 September when the library is ransacked by soldiers and the librarian is arrested, along with many other leftist young men. In the end, we hear the narrator speaking over the images of people being brought to prison: 'I think in those September days, my childhood ended, I began to grow up.' Among all the nostalgia films, *Vizontele Tuuba* most explicitly establishes the connection between the intervention of the central government in the local community and the idea of the end of childhood.

My Father and My Son not only became an enormous box-office success, but also gained fame as a phenomenal tear-jerker. Drawing upon favorite themes of Yeşilçam melodrama, such as the parent–child relationship, the film led to heated debates in the media on its release in 2005. Even the most aloof viewers confessed that they cried while watching it.

In the opening sequence of *My Father and My Son*, we see the protagonist trying in vain to find a taxi to take his pregnant wife to the hospital in the deserted streets of Istanbul during the curfew on the morning of 12 September 1980. His wife eventually dies on the street after giving birth to a baby boy. Later, the protagonist himself, a journalist, is arrested because of his leftist publications. On his release a few years later, he finds out that he has developed a fatal lung disease as a result of the torture to which he had been subjected in prison. Knowing that he will die soon, he takes his five-year-old son to his father's farm in a town on the Aegean coast. The rest of the story shows the painful process of reconciliation between the protagonist and his father, mostly from the grandchild's viewpoint. At first, the authoritarian father remains resentful and unforgiving. He blames his son for choosing a rebellious lifestyle instead of taking over the family business, but gradually he softens. However, by the time he can accept his son for who he is, it is too late. At the end of the film, the father embraces his grandson to help himself survive the pain of losing his son. As background to this melodramatic story, the film depicts a cheerful community life. Colored by a heavy regional accent, the comic moments in the film usually arise from the peculiar mode of speech of the characters, who constantly make fun of one another in a sarcastic, yet friendly tone. The intervening outside force in the film is the 1980 coup that devastates a family by taking away their son.

The International is set in 1982 Adıyaman, an eastern Anatolian town. During the period of martial law following the 1980 coup, commanders recruit a group of local street musicians to form a 'modern orchestra' that will perform music during commemoration ceremonies. The story centers on the conductor of this phony orchestra, Abuzer (Cezmi Baskın), and his family. Abuzer's daughter, Gülendam (Özgü Namal), flirts with a young university student of leftist leanings. The young lovers participate in secret activities, such as reading 'illegal' books (Engels' *The Origin of the Family*, for example) or listening to the famous socialist anthem, the 'Internationale.' Getting caught by her father while recording the 'Internationale,' Gülendam does not reveal what the song is actually about, but presents it as an ordinary melody. Later, the commanders decide to organize a special welcome ceremony for the members of the military council, the generals who staged the coup, who will visit the town soon. To please the commanders, Abuzer presents the tune of the 'Internationale' as his own composition and proposes to play it during the welcoming ceremony. Not knowing that the song in fact is a universal emblem of the international socialist movement, the commanders welcome this idea. Meanwhile, Gülendam also has a special plan for the ceremony. To make her boyfriend happy, she produces a huge colorful banner with a slogan protesting at the coup. On the day of the ceremony, the banner opens and the orchestra begins to play the 'Internationale.' Assuming that they are confronted with a hazardous protest, the members of the council abruptly leave. Panicking in the face of this unexpected turn of events, soldiers fire into the crowd. Gülendam's boyfriend is killed, and the members of the orchestra are arrested. During the investigation, Abuzer, in order to protect his daughter, insists that the 'Internationale' is his own composition. He dies in custody.

In nostalgia films, the provincial town-life of the past is viewed as a lost paradise. While the stories emphasize the warmth of human relations from a humorous as well as a sentimental viewpoint, the *mise-en-scène* is often dominated by aestheticized images of the rural landscape. Merging elements of comedy and melodrama, the two favorite genres of Yeşilçam cinema, popular nostalgia films attribute a sense of innocence to traditional community relations. The story usually ends at a moment when the state of innocence is about to be irrecoverably lost due to the intervention of an external force.

The thematic preoccupations of nostalgia films – imagining the past as collective childhood, critiquing the current social order through an idealized image of the past, and the association of malice with the intervention of outside forces – can sometimes also be observed in those films whose stories are set in the present. *The Bandit (Eşkıya*, Yavuz Turgul, 1996), the film that started the popular track of the new wave cinema in 1996, can actually be considered a nostalgia film of this sort.

The film tells the story of a Kurdish bandit who is released from prison after having served a thirty-five-year sentence. Upon his release, the bandit finds his village in eastern Anatolia partly submerged under the waters of a new dam. He also finds out that it was his best friend who turned him in, in order to marry the bandit's fiancée. An old woman, the sole remaining inhabitant of his village, gives him an amulet that will protect him from bullets, hence turning him into a mythic hero. On his way to Istanbul to find his fiancée, the bandit befriends a young man, a drug dealer whose life revolves around nightclubs and gambling joints. After they arrive in Istanbul, where they witness the harsh realities of poverty, violence, and alienation, the two develop a father–son relationship. The bandit eventually finds his fiancée; he finds out that she has refused to speak for years since she was forced to marry a man whom she does not love. The two plan to leave Istanbul together. However, the bandit has to sacrifice his love to protect his young friend, who gets into trouble with the mafia. In the end, the young man is killed, and the bandit begins a crusade to revenge his death. He himself is shot by the police in the last scene, after the amulet breaks and fails to protect him

The Bandit voices a tacit critique of the rapid transformation of Turkish society over the last two decades. Through the pro-tagonist's touching and tragicomic story, *The Bandit* posits the traditional values of honesty, heroism, and honor represented by the aging Kurdish bandit against the rising neo-liberal values of the 1990s. Istanbul is depicted as a locus of brutal capitalist rela-tions, relentless materialism, and cultural degeneration, whereas the rural east becomes the idealized site of an imaginary home. The film evokes a nostalgic yearning for the past through its hero, who represents and belongs to a different time and space.

II

Recent critical theory has suggested that memory is always active, constructed and situated in the present. In the words of Andreas Huyssen, 'rather than leading us to some authentic origin or giving us verifiable access to the real, memory [. . .] is itself based on representation. The past is not simply there in memory, but it must be articulated to become memory' (1995: 2). Cultural memory, in this sense, is something that is actually performed, even if such acts are not consciously or willfully contrived (Bal, 1999: vii).

How, then, can we characterize the peculiar act of memory that Turkish nostalgia films produce? How can we make sense of the persistent efforts of the new popular cinema to return to the past? What does the peculiar representation of the past in these films tell us about the present condition of Turkish society? How can we account for the enormous popularity of nostalgia films in Turkey? What kind of cultural memory is performed in these films, and which of its aspects appeal to the audience?

Over the last two decades, memory has become a major cultural obsession across the globe (Huyssen, 2003). In line with this trend, a culture of memory has been on the rise in Turkey since the 1990s. The emerging memory culture in Turkey strikes many as surprising since Turkish society is frequently accused of being amnesiac. Social scientists often claim that the Turkish Republic was originally based on forgetting (Özyürek, 2007: 3); in 1923, the newly founded Turkish Republic committed itself to a modernist future by erasing the memory of its immediate Ottoman past. Whereas the population of the Ottoman Empire was multi-religious, multi-ethnic, and multi-lingual, the Turkish nationalist movement came to identify itself primarily with the Turkish-speaking Muslim population. In this sense, the Turkish Republic was established on the assumption that the plural cultural legacy of the Ottoman Empire must be forgotten in order to create a singular national identity (Neyzi, 2002: 153). In the 1990s, almost eighty years after the establishment of the Republic, Turkish citizens began to develop a different relationship to the notion of memory. The growing interest in genres such as autobiography, the historical novel, and neighborhood and regional history during this period reflects a new concern with the past on the part of individuals. The multiple representations of the past with which they engage allow contemporary Turkish citizens to create alternative identities for themselves and their communities (Özyürek, 2007: 2). At the same time, the new interest in the past has become rapidly depoliticized, trivialized, and commodified (Neyzi, 2002: 142). While a nostalgia industry has emerged, nostalgia commodities allow people to reconnect with a past that has already vanished. Popular nostalgia films can be seen as part of this new culture of memory in Turkey. Drawing upon regional cultures and local communities, these films enable the audience to revisit their own past and consider new ways of representing their cultural identity.

Despite their generally light-hearted mood, nostalgia films do have a political stance. They attempt to critique contemporary Turkish society through an idealized representation of the past. They seem to suggest that Turkey's current problems arise from the unnecessary and often violent intrusion of the central government upon communal life. These intrusions have ultimately destroyed internal harmony and peace in Turkish society. The social critique that nostalgia films voice is problematic in the sense that they seek to resolve the tensions, anxieties, and contradictions that arise from complex social and political processes within a simple dichotomous structure based on before/after and inside/outside. In this structure, while malice is externalized, the presumed innocence and integrity of the 'inside,' of 'home,' is left intact. In this regard, the emphasis of nostalgia films is not so much on social memory, but on the imagining of the past as collective childhood. In these films, the provincial town-life of the past is transformed into an image of the felicitous space of childhood.

Pointing to the enormous popularity of child heroes in the history of Turkish popular culture – such as child actors in Yeşilçam cinema and child singers in arabesque music – Nurdan Gürbilek (2001), a prominent Turkish cultural critic, addresses Turkish society's tendency to identify itself with the image of an 'ill-fated child' and to derive pleasure from the self-pity arising from this image. According to Gürbilek, after the 12 September 1980 coup, Turkish society once again found itself in the position of a helpless child in the face of an unjust political authority and saw its own reflection in the images of suffering (and often orphaned) children. I would like to suggest that, unlike the child heroes in

40

Turkish popular culture, nostalgia films reproduce the much-cherished image of the ill-fated child not in the child characters, but in childish adults. These films infantilize adult characters in their representation of the provincial town-life of the past. While the recent past is represented as a period of collective childhood, society is turned into an ill-fated child in these films, a child that is vulnerable and helpless in the face of the external forces threatening its integrity. Equating childishness with innocence, nostalgia films render society unaccountable for the events of the past and save it from the burden of responsibility. Rather than engaging in a critical interrogation of the past, Turkish nostalgia films attempt to arrest the past in an image of frozen childhood.

III

Having made the above assertion, however, one should also acknowledge that such an analysis may not always fully capture the elusive character of nostalgia films. Not building their story around dramatic tension, nostalgia films often create a mood flavored with a peculiar blend of melancholy and humor. Their stories tend to emphasize secondary themes, minor characters, and inconsequential details. While yearning for a lost past is an immanent theme in these films, the nature of the loss is never clearly disclosed.

The term 'nostalgia' denotes longing for a home that no longer exists or has never existed. As such, nostalgia is a relation to the past often criticized for being unproductive, escapist, and sentimental (Bal, 1999: xi). Nostalgia, however, might have different forms that take on different values depending on the context. Talking about different forms of nostalgia, Svetlana Boym (2001) defines 'reflective nostalgia' as a mode cherishing the imperfect process of remembrance and shattered fragments of memory. The reflective mode of nostalgia puts emphasis not on the idea of recovering a loss or restoring a lost home, but on the very process of longing itself. Often ironic and humorous, it dwells upon ambivalences of longing and belonging (Boym, 2001: xviii). The most interesting moments in Turkish nostalgia films, I suggest, are the ones that invoke a mode of nostalgia that points to the ambivalences of longing and belonging. These ambivalent moments often appear in the marginal details and secondary themes of the stories.

To illustrate this point, I would like to focus on the ending of *Offside*, on the sequence depicting the funeral of the coach. At the end of the film, it is revealed that the coach, Hacı (Savaş Dinçel), is of Armenian origin. This revelation comes as a surprise to both the characters in the film and the audience. Hacı's closest friends apparently had no idea about his ethnic identity, in spite of all the years they spent together.

After Hacı's unexpected death, his friends send a telegram to an acquaintance of his in Istanbul, but do not receive a response. As a result, his friends in town organize Hacı's funeral, since he has no family and relatives. After the funeral services, conducted in accordance with traditional Muslim ritual, Hacı's friends gather in a local coffee-shop to dwell on their loss. Later, Hacı's acquaintance suddenly arrives from Istanbul, and, during the conversation he reveals that he is not just an acquaintance, but indeed Hacı's older brother. Embarrassed, the team members apologetically explain that they organized the funeral services themselves since they had assumed that Hacı did not have any living family members. Laughing loudly at this statement, the brother explains that their family is actually of Armenian (hence, Christian) origin; thus, it is ironic that Hacı was buried according to Islamic tradition. Hacı's friends are shocked at this revelation and ask what they should do now. 'Hacı was a good man,' the brother says, 'such things wouldn't bother him.' Then, they all go to Hacı's favorite restaurant to drink *rakı* (aniseed-flavored liquor) in his memory.

This sequence, I suggest, introduces a fundamental ambivalence to the text. On the one hand, it is possible to read the soft and gentle tone of the sequence in a sympathetic way. It seems that, although the recognition of cultural difference creates a shock effect at first, it then gives rise to tolerance and acceptance. Cultural difference, in other words, melts into a broader vision of the common faith of all of humanity. Such a soft and sympathetic approach to cultural difference is quite prominent in popular nostalgia films. *Vizontele* and *Vizontele Tuuba*, for example, make use of Kurdish identity only as a decorative element. Both films are set in a small town in eastern Anatolia, a region typically populated by people of Kurdish origin, but – although the films make reference to Kurdish culture in their use of music, costume, and proper names – Kurdish identity is never invoked as a political issue. At first glance, *Offside* seems to deploy a similar strategy, in the sense that it turns the question of cultural difference into a playful and humorous element in the narrative.

On another level, however, there is something deeply disturbing in this scene, in the sense that it makes us understand the coach's ordeal of having to conceal his identity for most of his life. Hacı, 'for some reason,' could not reveal his Armenian origins even to his closest friends in town and spent his entire life in secrecy and silence. This bizarre situation obviously has to do with Turkey's painful history in regard to its non-Muslim minorities. The histories of nation-state formation, Ayşe Gül Altınay (2007) states, are simultaneously histories of violence. The necessary homogenization and standardization that the nation-state requires always come at a high human cost:

> In Turkey, starting with the final years of the Ottoman Empire, which coincided with the Balkan Wars and the First World War, the transition from a multi-ethnic, multi-religious, multi-cultural empire to a 'Turkish' nation-state was a very painful one. For some communities, such as the Armenians of the Ottoman Empire, it means massive destruction to such an extent that Armenian life in Anatolia became virtually extinct. (Altınay, 2007: 23).

As a result of such policies, the number of religious minorities in the country has dramatically decreased. The remaining members of non-Muslim communities are often treated as potential outsiders in Republican Turkey, experiencing discrimination and encouragement (if not force) to emigrate (Neyzi, 2002: 140). Performing Turkishness, citizens of non-Muslim origin feel the need to hide alternative histories from the public sphere, and sometimes the familial as well (Neyzi, 2002: 138). Keeping silent about their past has become a viable strategy of survival for the members of non-Muslim communities in a potentially volatile political environment. Hacı, in *Offside*, presumably chooses to conceal his ethnic identity in order to pass for a 'real' Turkish citizen in a small provincial town. Considering the story retrospectively in the light of this information, we can now make better sense of the melancholic side of the character's personality and the perpetual sense of loss from which he suffers.

Offside, then, hints at the dark underside of collective childishness. Beneath the appearance of a harmonious community life, the film seems to imply, there lies the silencing of cultural difference. The fantasy of belonging to a closed, intimate, family-like community comes at a cost. Collective childishness seems to be possible only at the expense of denial, forgetting, and suppression. The idealized home of childhood turns into a spectral house in the film, haunted by silenced memories. Dwelling upon ambivalences of longing and belonging, *Offside* is an account of reflective nostalgia.

IV

Although nostalgia films generally evoke a reflective mode of longing for the past, a different form of nostalgia is not altogether absent in contemporary Turkish cinema. This is the 'restorative nostalgia' that Svetlana Boym (2001) contrasts with the reflective mode. As opposed to the reflective nostalgia that concerns individual memory, restorative nostalgia evokes a national past and proposes to rebuild the lost home. Not considering itself nostalgic, restorative nostalgia maintains that its project is about truth (Boym, 2001: 41). The two dominant narrative plots of restorative nostalgia are the restoration of origins and conspiracy theory. 'This kind of nostalgia,' writes Boym, 'characterizes national and nationalist revivals all over the world, which engage in the anti-modern myth-making of history by means of a return to national symbols and myths and, occasionally, through swapping conspiracy theories' (2001: 41).

The Valley of the Wolves Iraq (*Kurtlar Vadisi Irak*, Serdar Akar, 2006), arguably the most controversial Turkish film of the time due to its politically charged story and enthusiastic reception, is a typical example of the conspiratorial worldview of restorative nostalgia. Based on a hit television series with the same title, the film broke the box-office and film budget records, as we have already seen.

The enormous popularity of *Valley of the Wolves Iraq* must be understood in the context of the rising popularity of nationalist discourses in Turkey over the last two decades. Established during a grave crisis in which its very existence was threatened, Tanıl Bora (2003) argues, modern Turkey has a nation-state tradition that has subsequently perceived surrounding countries as a serious threat. This condition of survival and threat has had a considerable effect on the way in which Turkish nationalism and the Turkish national identity have taken shape (Bora, 2003: 434). The strengthening of nationalist discourses in Turkey since the 1990s can be seen as an outcome of a series of developments. The rise of the Kurdish separatist movement and the armed clashes between the Turkish army and Kurdish guerillas was one major factor leading to the rise of nationalism. Having claimed the lives of an estimated 30,000 people, mostly of Kurdish origin, the protracted conflict in eastern Anatolia also led to the surfacing of a 'deep-state' formation in Turkey, which refers to the 'corrupt and repressive state implicated in mafia business and authoritarian politics' (Robins and Aksoy, 2000: 203).

The second development that strengthened nationalism was the improving relations between Turkey and the European Union in the 1990s. As already mentioned, following the official announcement of Turkey's candidacy for the EU membership at the 1999 Helsinki Summit, the steps taken in the process towards Turkey's full membership to the EU caused alarm among the state elite in Ankara. This was because, as Çağlar Keyder (2004) explains, the reforms required by the EU demanded significant changes to the national security system and its ideological props:

> The ideal of nation as community would have to yield to rule of law; enforcement of civil and political liberties would strengthen oppositional forces. The cultural rights of the Kurdish minority would have to be recognized, and secularism redefined to allow freedom of religious organization and expression. Perhaps most controversial, the military would have to abdicate its regency over the state. (Keyder, 2004: 80)

Accordingly, opposition to the European project mobilized a nationalist movement to defend the unitary and sovereign national structure against European demands (Keyder, 2004: 80). Finally, the aggressive expansionist policy of the United States during the post-9/11 era and the consequent instability in the Middle East fostered nationalist discourses in Turkey. The Turkish public disapproved of the US invasion of Iraq in 2003 and the subsequent atrocities committed by US soldiers. All these developments contributed not only to the rise of nationalist discourses in Turkey, but also to a certain mode of conspiratorial and paranoid thinking.

The phenomenon of *Valley of the Wolves* (both the television series and the film) can be seen as an outcome of the rising nationalist discourses shaped around a conspiratorial and paranoid mentality. In an interview, Osman Sınav, the producer and director of the television series, has argued that Turkey needed such a film, since the geography of the country is like a valley running from Europe to the Middle East and the Caucasus: 'Turkey takes place in the world's valley of the wolves,' he stated, 'what happens here must be deciphered.'[5] Telling the story of dark relations between a group of Turkish intelligence service agents and members of Turkish and international mafia organizations, *Valley of the Wolves* is a mafia drama series presenting the geopolitical location of Turkey as a territory where superpowers have historically confronted each other to expand their economic and political interests. Located in a historically volatile territory, Turkey is imagined to be under the constant threat of various malicious forces.

Valley of the Wolves Iraq, the film sequel to the television drama series, narrates the adventures of a Turkish intelligence agent who goes to northern Iraq on a special mission to take revenge for an assault against Turkish soldiers by American warlords. The beginning of the story is based on a 'true event.' On 4 July 2003, US forces entered the unofficial Turkish headquarters in northern Iraq and deported the eleven Turkish soldiers stationed there, blindfolding them with hoods. In the fictional part of the film, one of these soldiers leaves behind a letter before committing suicide. This letter is addressed to Polat Alemdar (Necati Şaşmaz), a specially trained Turkish intelligence agent. Polat Alemdar, who at this point has no official ties to the Intelligence Agency, cannot ignore the last wish of his friend and goes to northern Iraq with his two men. There, he begins a crusade against the man who insulted the Turkish soldiers, Sam William Marshall (Billy Zane), a Special Forces commander. Constituting an ironic contrast to the anti-American sentiments that the film voices, the protagonist of *Valley of the Wolves Iraq*, nick-named 'Turkish Rambo,' is an American-style action hero. He is all-powerful, undefeatable and devotedly patriotic.

According to Boym, 'The conspiratorial worldview reflects a nostalgia for a transcendental cosmology and a simple pre-modern conception of good and evil' (2001: 43); there is no room for ambivalence in this conspiratorial worldview. As modern history is seen as a fulfillment of ancient prophecy, the complexity of history and the specificity of modern circumstances are erased (Boym, 2001: 43). *Valley of the Wolves Iraq* operates within a similar conspiratorial worldview. The film's critical position towards the US invasion of Iraq is grounded not in a historically informed understanding of politics, but in a trans-historical plot based on a Manichaean battle of good and evil. The USA represents the unmistakable evil in this battle, with its sadistic soldiers killing civilians for sport, perverted doctors dealing in human organs, and sinister warlords and missionaries preoccupied with the idea of taking the region under Western and Christian domination. Iraqi Kurdish leaders are portrayed as ignorant yet greedy actors, blindly obeying the Americans. Iraqi Turks take the role of victims forced by the Kurds to leave their homeland so that the ethnic make-up of northern Iraq will change in favor of the Kurdish population. Polat Alemdar is inserted into this picture as a reincarnation of the Ottoman/Turkish legacy, presumably representing the ultimate 'good' party. The idealized image of his position is made manifest in the suicide note of the Turkish soldier. 'Apart from our ancestors,' the soldier states in his letter, 'all the powers who reigned here tyrannized the people of this land.' Seen as a symbol of a glorious past, the Ottoman rule is idealized in this view as the sole 'good' power in history, ruling the territories from the Middle East to the Balkans without tyrannizing the people. In fact, this is precisely what contemporary Turkish nationalism is nostalgic about: the long-lost Ottoman/Turkish imperial power. This is also the type of nostalgia that prevails in *Valley of the Wolves Iraq*. The film appeals to the nationalist fantasy of 'restoring' Ottoman/Turkish imperial power in the Middle East.

V

Svetlana Boym (2001: 41) contends that different modes of nostalgia should not be taken as absolute types; rather, they should be seen as ways of giving shape and meaning to longing. Reflective and restorative nostalgia, in this regard, are not necessarily contradictory types, but rather continuous modes that can easily give way to one another. *Offside* and *Valley of the Wolves Iraq* actually constitute an ironic manifestation of this assertion, since they are both made by the same director, Serdar Akar.

Although they seem to be articulated from different ideological positions (left-wing opposition versus conservative nationalist), it is possible to discern a subtle continuity between popular nostalgia films such as *Offside* and *Valley of the Wolves Iraq*, in the sense that they both end up in a romantic and celebratory vision of belonging that precludes a candid account of the past. Facing the experienced past, Leyla Neyzi writes, means 'facing up to the violence experienced in this society during this century – whether between the state and particular communities, between communities, between generations, or within the individual psyche itself. It means confronting the exclusionary aspects of national identity, and its high cost for individuals' (2002: 142). Drawing upon a romantic fantasy of belonging, popular nostalgia films cannot handle such a facing up to the past. This challenging task is taken up by new political films.

2

NEW POLITICAL FILMS

As a result of the process of democratization over the last decade, Turkish cinema has begun to address politically charged issues more easily than before. To a certain extent, this new liberal atmosphere is an outcome of the improving relations between Turkey and the European Union from the late 1990s to the early 2000s. The relative softening of political censorship since the mid-1980s also has had a positive impact on Turkish cinema.

Censorship has always been an important problem for Turkish cinema (Erdoğan and Göktürk, 2001). Until the mid-1980s, censorship was a matter for the police. There was no law regulating the production, distribution, exhibition, or importation of films in Turkey until the mid-1930s. Despite the absence of legal regulations, however, the city governors of the Ministry of the Interior were fully authorized to deal with the matter (Erdoğan and Göktürk, 2001: 539). In 1934, the Regulation on the Control of Films and Film Screenplays was formulated as part of the Police Duty and Authorization Law, and it was applied with minor revisions until 1977. On the basis of this regulation, the Board of Censors examined screenplays prior to the production of the film. On the basis of their examination, they might authorize a film, ban it, or request revisions. Apart from this procedure, the Ministry of the Interior reserved the right to censor or ban a film, even if it had been approved by the Board of Censors. This censorship procedure prevented filmmakers from promoting challenging ideas or developing any explicit social or political critique (Erdoğan and Göktürk, 2001: 540). In 1977, the law was reformulated in such a way as to express concern for the mental health of juvenile audiences and loosely suggest a rating system be introduced. This censorship procedure remained intact until the mid-1980s despite efforts to change it. The Ministry of Culture became responsible for affairs of censorship starting in 1986, which brought about considerable relaxation (Erdoğan and Göktürk, 2001).

As a result of the process of democratization and the relative softening of political censorship, potentially inflammatory subjects such as the periods of martial law, discriminatory policies against religious minorities, or the conflict with Kurdish separatist guerillas in the southeast have been critically interrogated in the films of the last decade. Although a number of films made during this period addressed important political issues, I believe that several of these works deserve special attention, since they do not merely include political subjects in their stories, but also employ an innovative cinematic style in dealing with them. *Journey to the Sun* (*Güneşe Yolculuk*, Yeşim Ustaoğlu, 1999), *In Nowhere Land* (*Hiçbiryerde*, Tayfun Pirselimoğlu, 2002), *Mud* (*Çamur*, Derviş Zaim, 2003), *Waiting for the Clouds* (*Bulutları Beklerken*, Yeşim Ustaoğlu, 2003), and *Toss Up* (*Yazı/Tura*, Uğur Yücel, 2004) are the films that can be listed among the most interesting examples of new political cinema.

The past we encounter in new political films is not nostalgic, but quite traumatic. The spectral home at the center of the new political cinema is haunted by the traumatic events of the past. As opposed to the evasive tendency of popular nostalgia films whose engagement with politics usually does not go beyond a light-hearted handling of social problems within the conventions of dark comedy, new political cinema overtly tackles history and politics. New political films typically focus attention on how the lives of ordinary people have been destroyed by the turbulent political climate of Turkey during the recent past. The dialectic of remembering and forgetting is central to the stories. Without endorsing a single position or offering clear-cut solutions, new political films are preoccupied with the question of how to come to terms with a traumatic past. In doing so, they render the questions of national belonging and identity problematic.

I

While the notion of journey is a major thematic preoccupation of new political films, the narrative dynamic is always generated by a sense of loss. Stories revolve around real or imagined journeys that the characters embark upon to cope with the loss from which they suffer.

Among the films that I discuss in this chapter, *Journey to the Sun*, *In Nowhere Land*, and *Toss Up* draw upon the traumatic consequences of the armed conflict between the Turkish army and the separatist Kurdish guerillas in southeastern Turkey, whereas *Mud* and *Waiting for the Clouds* deal with rarely explored political issues: the dilemmas of Turkish-Cypriot identity, and the suppression of non-Muslim minorities in the history of the Republic, respectively.

Journey to the Sun tells the story of a friendship between two young men who have recently migrated to Istanbul from different parts of Turkey for different reasons. Berzan (Nazmi Kırık), a Kurdish man from eastern Anatolia, has to leave his village for political reasons after his father was taken by soldiers one night and disappeared. Afraid that he might end up like his father, Berzan leaves his village. He works as a street-peddler selling tape cassettes in the Eminönü district of Istanbul and lives in a squatter's house on the outskirts of the city. Mehmet

Mehmet (Newroz Baz) in *Journey to the Sun*
(*Güneşe Yolculuk*, Yeşim Ustaoğlu, 1999)

(Newroz Baz), on the other hand, comes to Istanbul from Tire,
a western Anatolian town, for employment. He has a small
job with the city's water department and shares a poor hostel
room with other young working-class men. Because of his dark
skin color and dark hair, people often assume Mehmet to be of
Kurdish origin. Unlike Berzan, who is politically aware and close
to the Kurdish cause, Mehmet seems to be quite disinterested in
political issues. One day, while traveling on a minibus, a bag is
left next to him by a passenger who runs off upon seeing a police
checkpoint. The bag contains a gun. Mehmet is arrested and
roughed up by police during a week of interrogation. Upon his
release, he is evicted from the hostel and fired by his employer
because of the arrest. Berzan helps him find employment and
provides shelter. During the time they spend together, the
friendship between the two young men deepens. Berzan tells

Mehmet how much he longs for his homeland and his fiancée whom he left behind; his dream is to return to his village one day. Eventually, Berzan is killed in a demonstration protesting at the conditions endured by political prisoners. Devastated by the loss of his friend, Mehmet's only wish from that point on is to take Berzan's body back to his village to be buried in his own homeland. The rest of the film follows Mehmet's long journey from Istanbul all the way to Zorduç, with Berzan's coffin by his side. As he observes the oppressive political atmosphere prevailing in eastern Turkey throughout his journey, Mehmet is gradually transformed. When he finally reaches Berzan's village, he is a different person.

In Nowhere Land tells the story of a journey, that of a mother looking for her missing son. Working at the ticket office of the central train station in Istanbul, Şükran (Zuhal Olcay) is a middle-aged widow living a modest life with her young son, Veysel, whom we never see in the film. One day Veysel does not return home. Applying to the Missing Persons Bureau in desperation, Şükran at first is in complete denial of the possibility that the disappearance of Veysel might have to do with his political affiliations. Having suffered from her husband's political dealings in the past, she has tried very hard to bring up Veysel in such a way as to keep him away from any political influences. Now, however, it seems that her efforts have failed and that Veysel probably has connections to the separatist Kurdish movement. Hearing by chance from a police officer that Veysel has last been seen in Mardin, the birthplace of his father, Şükran embarks on a journey to eastern Turkey for the first time in her life. Never losing faith that Veysel is still alive, she finds herself within a network of secretive relationships and a fearful atmosphere in Mardin. As her attempts to find Veysel fail one by one, she gradually comes to admit that Veysel might have been killed because of his political leanings. When she finally returns to her lonely flat in Istanbul, she is an anguished, yet more sober and aware woman.

One of the most debated films of the recent years, *Toss Up* takes a look at the devastating consequences of the war in southeastern Turkey from the perspective of veteran soldiers. The story is about two young men who by chance serve their obligatory military duty together in the southeast and were wounded during a clash with Kurdish guerillas. The narrative is composed of two parts, each part telling the home-coming story of one of the men after their discharge from the army in 1999. Having lost a leg in a landmine explosion, Rıdvan (Olgun Şimşek) returns to his hometown, Göreme, in central Anatolia. Contrary to his expectations, he is not welcomed as a war hero by the townspeople, but seen as someone pitiable. Once a local football player, he now does not know what to do with himself. He is betrayed by his fiancée, who has begun a relationship with his closest friend in his absence. Finding refuge in alcohol and drugs, his life seems to be lost in oblivion. In the second part, we see the story of Cevher (Kenan İmirzalıoğlu), who has gone deaf in his right ear as a result of the same explosion that injured Rıdvan. He returns to Istanbul with plans to set up a railroad-platform snack bar, but his plans go wrong after the Marmara earthquake. After the disaster, his long-lost stepbrother returns from Greece. Discovering that his brother is gay, Cevher goes through the painful process of facing his own weaknesses that lie behind his macho tough guy appearance. In the end, he kills someone for insulting his brother and goes to jail.

Mud takes up the issue of Cypriot-Turkish identity, a subject that had never been addressed in Turkish cinema before. Through a portrayal of a group of middle-aged friends, it gives an account of the traumatizing effects of the period of violence between Greek and Turkish Cypriots in 1974 and the subsequent process of partition. Ali (Mustafa Uğurlu), the central character of the film, loses his voice due to an undiagnosed disease during the last weeks of his compulsory military service, which he belatedly serves in his forties. The type of marsh plant that grows around the dried salt lake next to which Ali stands guard at a checkpoint is believed to cure many types of disease. Applying mud to his throat in the hope of finding a remedy for his mysterious loss of voice, Ali gradually becomes obsessed with mud. When he searches for mud inside a well one day, he discovers an ancient sculpture of a fertility goddess. Turning out to be a precious archeological find, the sculpture will eventually bring destruction to Ali and everyone around him. As the background to this story, the film portrays the different attitudes that the characters develop to cope with the past. The dried lake is actually the area around which Ali's friends killed their Greek neighbors in 1974 in order to take revenge for the massacre of their relatives and fellow Turkish villagers by Greeks. The memory of this unspeakable crime haunts them today in different ways. Ali's loss of voice seems to be a psychosomatic symptom as a reaction to the resurfacing of the past. Temel (Taner Birsel), who believes that the painful memories of the past can be cured only through dialogue, is a peace activist and tries to find ways to get Greek and Turkish Cypriots to communicate with each other. Thinking that such attempts are pointless, Halil (Bülent Yarar) is preoccupied with the idea of getting rich and starting a new life. In the end, all three men are killed by smugglers of archeological finds who wish to get hold of Ali's sculpture.

Waiting for the Clouds opens with census clerks arriving in the small port-town of Tirebolu in the Black Sea region in the late 1970s. Ayşe/Eleni (Rüçhan Çalışkur), the main character of the film, is an old woman living with her sick elderly stepsister. Ayşe becomes anxious when the clerks want to see her official identification card, since she actually is not of 'Turkish origin,' but the daughter of a Pontic Greek family evacuated from the region in 1916. Ayşe's true identity is a secret that she and her beloved sister have kept throughout their entire lives. That day, the two women manage to conceal Ayşe's identity from the census control. Not long after, the older sister passes away and

Ayşe is left all alone. Withdrawing to her tiny wooden cabin in the mountains, she slowly isolates herself from everyone and spends her days watching the movements of the clouds. The only person who can approach her is the eight-year-old neighbor boy. After days in silence, Ayşe gradually begins to talk in Greek, a language that the boy cannot understand. In long monologue scenes, she tells the painful story of the forced evacuation of her family along with other villagers of Greek origin from the land where they were born. She narrates how they spent days walking southwards barefoot, how hundreds of people around her, including her own parents, died of hunger and disease on this journey. Eleni survived this traumatic incident, because she was rescued by a benevolent Turkish family, who later adopted her. Eleni's younger brother, meanwhile, joined a group of Greek villagers who escaped by taking refuge on a Russian boat. Not having the courage to follow her brother, Eleni never hears from him again. In the end, Ayşe/Eleni travels to Greece to look for her younger brother and to make peace with her past. When she finally finds him in Thessaloniki, however, she experiences not a warm reunion, but bitterness and disappointment.

II

New political films decidedly focus on the traumatic events of Turkey's recent history and disclose how the subjectivity of the characters is shaped around a sense of loss generated by traumatic experiences. Recent studies on 'traumatic memory' suggest that traumatic events of the past persist in the present. The concept of traumatic memory, in fact, is regarded as a misnomer, since traumatic memories never belong to the past, but remain present for the subject with particular vividness (Bal, 1999: viii). For the characters in new political films, the past is arrested in the present. The 'house,' in this regard, turns into a potent figure embodying the persistence of the traumatic past in the present.

New political films are populated by the images of eerie houses haunted by the ghosts of the past. The spectral home at the center of these films indeed has quite a material presence.

In *Journey to the Sun*, the figure of the spectral home gains a material presence during Mehmet's journey to eastern Turkey. As he drives his decrepit van through the vast landscape, he comes to a deserted town. During the armed conflict in southeastern Turkey between 1984 and 1999, a large wave of internal displacement took place, since the Kurdish inhabitants of many rural settlements were evicted. The town where Mehmet stops is one of these emptied settlements, which turns into a ghost town without its inhabitants. With their half-ruined walls and ripped-out window cases, the houses are like relics of a long-forgotten civilization. Mehmet steps into one of the abandoned houses, looks around the empty rooms for a minute, then, feeling uneasy, goes outside. After the character leaves, the camera remains inside for a while. Located at a low-angle stationary position in the corner of the room, the camera shows us the bare interior in the beam of light coming from the half-open door. Denying the audience any identification with the character's point of view, this is a fairly disturbing scene, making us feel the sense of void characterizing the space.

Mehmet comes across another ghost town at the end of his journey. After days of traveling, he finally arrives at Zorduç by horse-carriage one afternoon, only to find it under water. It is one of the many villages flooded because of a large dam project in southeastern Anatolia; the vision of the town is utterly surreal with a minaret half-covered by water, roofs peeking out, and electricity wires hanging slightly above the surface of the water. Dragging Berzan's coffin into the water, Mehmet takes his time to watch it floating first, then slowly sinking. In the background, a flock of pigeons circles in the air against the pink evening sky. The ghost towns in *Journey to the Sun* are like mute witnesses to violence, war, and the forced deportation that Kurdish people have experienced in southeastern Turkey over the last two decades. In their silent and resolute existence, these deserted spaces become an embodiment of the traumatic past.

Ghost towns in Turkey are not limited to the abandoned towns in southeastern Anatolia, and their history is actually much older than the history of the conflict with separatist Kurdish guerillas. Attila Durak, a Turkish photographer, speaks of the ghost towns of his childhood in northern Turkey as follows:

> I was born in Gümüşhane, which, like many cities in Anatolia, is located in a region that bears the traces of many cultures. The town got its name from the mine in the 'old city,' which produced the silver used in Ottoman coins. When I was a child, the 'old city' looked like a *ghost town*. It was hard to imagine that its streets were once filled with the sounds of Armenian tinsmiths swinging their hammers and Greek shopkeepers opening up their stores. Aided by the boundless imagination of childhood, we played on the deserted streets reveling in the 'ghostly' haunts left to us by a once vibrant community. (Durak, 2007: 13, emphasis added)

The process that led to the foundation of the Turkish nation-state included traumatic events during which religious minorities were massacred, deported, or encouraged to migrate in the name of establishing a homogeneous national identity (Altınay, 2007; Özyürek, 2007). As a result of such policies, religious minorities in the country decreased dramatically. Several ghost towns from which non-Muslim communities were evicted in earlier times are still found in different parts of Anatolia as remnants of a lost history.

Waiting for the Clouds evokes the figure of the ghost town without actually showing it. The main character's identity in the film is shaped around a rupture, the haunting memory of the forced evacuation she experienced with her family during her childhood. The episode that Ayşe/Eleni remembers in the film belongs to the turbulent period of the collapse of the Ottoman Empire. Having been at the crossroads of Greek and Turkish cultures for centuries, Tirebolu, the northern town where the story is set, witnessed a turbulent period during World War I.

In the words of historian Arzu Öztürkmen, 'although irregular migration had begun among the Greeks and Armenians of Tirebolu before the turn of the century, the more drastic experience of displacement came with the First World War, when exile policies touched the non-Muslim communities of the town and when simultaneously many Muslim families escaped to Western towns, fearing a Russian invasion' (Öztürkmen, 2006: 95). During this period, Greeks residing in villages near the Russian-occupied cities were forced to suffer hasty, haphazard, and deadly deportations by the Ottoman army. Eleni apparently survived deportation thanks to a benevolent family rescuing her. She has to pay a high price for survival, however, since she takes on a new name, Ayşe, and pretends throughout her adult life that she is the daughter of a Turkish family. The atonement for survival, in other words, is the suppression of her past and real identity. Now, after years of silence, Eleni begins to remember her long-lost childhood home. Where everyone sees the mundane realities of the present, she sees the ghosts of the past.

The figure of the spectral home takes on a different meaning in *Mud*. Ali, the main character, lives with his sister in an ostensibly ordinary place, a white, modestly decorated, one-story village house. Like hundreds of other houses in Cyprus, however, theirs is a house that used to belong to a Greek family before partition.

The political history of Cyprus is full of bizarre and often tragic contradictions that complicate the sense of belonging for its inhabitants. Having been part of the Ottoman territory for almost 250 years, Cyprus fell under the control of the United Kingdom and eventually became a British colony by the end of the nineteenth century. The island became an independent entity in 1960, while Britain, Greece, and Turkey were designated as the guarantors of its independence. Conflicts between Greek and Turkish Cypriots arose in 1963 and 1964, a forerunner of the period of violence that was to come in the early 1970s. On 15 July 1974, the Greek junta government organized a coup in Cyprus. Five days later, the Turkish army disembarked on the island and occupied one third of it. This led to the displacement of thousands of Cypriots and the establishment of a separate Turkish-Cypriot political entity in the north. Consequently, thousands of Greek Cypriots from the north became refugees in the south, while Turkish Cypriots of the south moved to the north. Until recently, there was no communication between the Greek and Turkish parts of Cyprus. In 2004, Cyprus was scheduled to join the European Union, and the UN-backed Annan Plan for Cyprus sought to reunify the island before the EU accession. The plan was put to civilians on both sides in separate referenda in April 2004. The Greek side overwhelmingly rejected the Annan Plan, while the Turkish side voted in favor. In May 2004, Cyprus entered the European Union, although in practice membership only applies to the southern part of the island, which is under the control of the Republic of Cyprus. In 2005, Turkish Cypriots demolished their part of the wall along the boundary that for decades had divided the island. In 2007, Greek Cypriots demolished the wall on the Greek side. In the period during which *Mud* was made, however, the communication between the Turkish and Greek parts of Cyprus had not yet begun.

So, in *Mud*, the ordinary-looking house that the main character inhabits is one of those houses that Greek villagers left behind after their forced deportation to the south. Because of the haphazard and often horrendous conditions of the eviction, families abandoned their homes without taking even their most precious personal belongings with them. Ali and his sister live in a house populated by the memories of a family whom they cannot meet since it is prohibited to cross to the other side. To overcome this surreal situation, Temel, a peace activist and amateur artist, develops several projects that aim to establish communication between Turkish and Greek Cypriots who live next to each other without ever getting in touch. One of his projects is to make realistic sculptures of the previous inhabitants of the houses on the basis of their video images and give them to the present inhabitants to be placed in their living rooms. Hence, a full-size plaster figure of an old man sits on the sofa in Ali's living room. At first appearing as an absurd decorative element, the sculpture actually functions as a disturbing reminder of a spectral past.

The figure of the spectral home in *In Nowhere Land* appears in the context of the problem of missing persons in Turkey. In the first part of the film, Şükran tries to find her missing son everywhere. She believes that his disappearance is a 'normal' disappearance and insists on following official procedure to find him. Still, she cannot get any reply from the authorities. There is no record of Veysel's arrest by the police, and the police do not explain his disappearance. They only show her the bodies of several murdered people for possible identification. In this sense, the story of the film is similar to the stories of the hundreds of missing persons who disappear while in police custody in Turkey. Often, there is no official record of the arrest of these persons, and the authorities do not take any responsibility. Starting after the 1980 military coup and intensifying throughout the 1990s, particularly in the war-stricken eastern regions, the phenomenon of missing persons has been one of the darkest pages of Turkey's recent history. Many who were summoned by the police during this period were declared 'missing while in custody.' Some of them were found dead later. Based on applications made to the Human Rights Watch, the number of missing persons was declared to be 543 by the year 2005, although the actual number is estimated to be much higher.[1]

In 1995, a group of mothers organized themselves around the Human Rights Association and initiated one of the most significant and publicized protest movements in Istanbul (Baydar and İvegen, 2006: 691). Every Saturday at midday, a group of mothers gathered at a central location in Istanbul and sat on the street to protest the disappearance of their children while in police custody. The protest lasted for 200

Saturdays, from 27 May 1995 to 13 March 1999, as the number of its participants increased from thirty to somewhere in the hundreds (Baydar and İvegen, 2006: 689). The media called the group 'Saturday Mothers.' In 1999, the mothers decided to discontinue the protest because the government's reactions were turning increasingly violent.

Şükran, the mother in *In Nowhere Land*, is not one of the Saturday Mothers. In fact, she distances herself from any kind of political activism and denies her son's possible political involvement. But Şule (Devin Özgür Çınar), Veysel's girlfriend, claims that she has identified Veysel's body in the morgue. To make Şükran accept her son's death, Şule takes her to a woman whose son was killed while in police custody. The film casts one of the actual Saturday Mothers in that role, and she gives a real account of the disappearance and subsequent death of her son. Getting angry at Şule for insisting that Veysel has been killed, Şükran wants to believe that her son is still alive. Thus, the film draws upon the unbearable indeterminacy of a missing loved one. Not knowing whether her son is dead or alive, the main character constantly oscillates between hope and desperation. The spectral home at the center of the film is the lonely flat of the mother, haunted by the memory of her missing son.

As described at the opening of this book, in one scene in the first part of *Toss Up*, Rıdvan regards the cave houses of his hometown after another alcoholic night and says in bewilderment: 'There are ghosts in those houses.' It is possible to consider this line on two levels. The denotative meaning obviously has to do with the marvels of the geographical landscape of Cappadocia, a central Anatolian region characterized by the so-called 'fairy chimneys,' conical rock formations formed by streams of lava from ancient volcanoes. An attractive tourist destination today, houses in Cappadocia are often carved from rock formations. With their startling curvy shapes, these houses have indeed a fairy-tale look that might make one think that they are haunted. Under the influence of alcohol and drugs,

Rıdvan seems to be hallucinating in the face of the startling geography of his hometown. There is more to the character's statement, however. The ghosts that he sees might also have to do with the traumatic memories of the war, which he cannot share with anyone. What is all too real and tangible for the character is not recognizable for others. Rıdvan's experience is in fact quite similar to that of thousands of others in Turkey who served their compulsory military duty in the southeast during the 1990s and had serious difficulties in readjusting to civil life after their release from the army.

While popular nationalist discourses in Turkey widely celebrate military service as men's sacred duty to their country, the traumatic experiences of soldiers involved in fighting with Kurdish guerillas in the southeast is a taboo subject never discussed in the public sphere. If a major migratory movement in Turkey during the 1990s has been one of Kurdish migration from the villages to the cities in the region and from the region to other parts of Turkey, observes Ayşe Gül Altınay, 'a reverse movement has been that of young men, mostly in their twenties, leaving their homes and families in other parts of Turkey and moving into the region to "fight against terrorism"' (1999: 131). Although there are no official figures on how many young men have become involved in this conflict, the number is usually estimated to be more than 2 million (Mater, 1999). Despite their large numbers, veterans have not become part of the debate on the war or the Kurdish issue in general, except when they die. The funerals of these 'martyrs' have been political venues, especially for those who want to condemn PKK actions (Altınay, 1999: 127). Those who return from the war alive are expected to keep their memories to themselves in order to keep the presumed sanctity of military service intact.

The taboo concerning the experiences of soldiers who were involved in the war in southeastern Turkey was first broken by independent journalist Nadire Mater's 1999 book, *Mehmedin Kitabı: Güneydoğu'da Savaşmış Askerler Anlatıyor* (*Mehmet's Book:*

Soldiers Who Have Fought in the Southeast Speak Out). The name Mehmet in the title comes from the generic name Mehmetçik, literally Little Mehmet, which is often used to refer to soldiers in a sympathetic way. Mater's book is based on interviews with forty-two former soldiers who participated in the fighting against the seperatist Kurdish guerillas during their compulsory military service between the years 1984 and 1998. The accounts of the soldiers reveal for the first time the horrific face of the war and its damaging effects on the psychology of those involved. Upon its publication by Metis Press in Istanbul, the book was banned. Mater and her publisher were tried under Article 159 of the penal code for insulting and belittling the military. The trial lasted for two years and resulted in the acquittal of the parties.[2]

Following in the footsteps of Mater's book, *Toss Up* is a groundbreaking film in the sense that it dares to shatter the myth of sacred military service and takes a genuine look at the experiences of those who were involved in the war in southeastern Turkey. For the two protagonists of the film, the trauma of the war cannot be left behind, but persists in their so-called 'civilian' life. Susan J. Brison (1999) contends that memories of traumatic events are often themselves traumatic, that is, uncontrollable, intrusive, and frequently somatic. They are experienced by the subject as inflicted, not chosen, flashbacks to the events themselves (Brison, 1999: 40). In *Toss Up*, the memory of the landmine explosion in which both men were wounded comes back to the characters in an intrusive way, as flashbacks. As if to mimic the traumatized vision of the characters, the movements of the hand-held camera in the film are always restless and shaky. Shot on DVD and then transferred to 35mm, the look of the film is generally flawed and disquieting. The second part especially creates a claustrophobic effect, as the camera is at times held at an annoyingly close distance from its subject. Reflecting the mental processes of its traumatized characters and representing reality obliquely, as seen through their eyes, *Toss Up* is indeed a trauma film, both in terms of its story and its unconventional cinematic style.[3]

It would be unfair, however, to take *Toss Up* as a film solely about the traumatizing effects of war on soldiers. The film raises unsettling questions about the ethical and political aspects of the war and reveals its destructive consequences on an entire society. The landmine explosion during which both characters were wounded was not an accident, but a self-inflicted destructive act on the part of Rıdvan. Through flashback sequences, the film presents fragmented details of this incident. The explosion, we learn, took place in the aftermath of a combat during which a group of Kurdish guerillas were killed. We see Turkish soldiers, Cevher and Rıdvan among them, early on a winter morning searching the dead bodies of Kurdish guerillas to find out their identities. At one point, Cevher, looking puzzled, approaches Rıdvan to say that he has found a picture of Rıdvan in the pocket of a female guerilla. Rıdvan goes to see the body, only to find out that it is that to Elif, his high-school sweetheart. Losing control, Rıdvan begins to run through the snow, frantically firing his automatic rifle into the air. Sensing that his friend is out of control, Cevher runs towards Rıdvan to stop him. It is too late, however: Rıdvan has already stepped on a landmine. Elif, the Kurdish female guerilla killed by Rıdvan, is the daughter of a family from Bingöl, a southeastern town. The traumatic loss that Rıdvan suffers from, therefore, is not only that of his bodily unity, but perhaps more significantly, that of the other. *Toss Up* seems to suggest that it is impossible to achieve an undisturbed sense of belonging without facing loss and mourning for it.

III

Although the traumatic events that the new political cinema puts forward are often related to questions of cultural difference and identity, the films decidedly avoid essentializing these notions. They approach belonging and identity not as a fixed essence, but as performative constructs. One does not simply or ontologically belong, asserts Vikki Bell (1999), to the world or to any group within it. Belonging is an achievement at several levels of abstraction and an effect of performance (Bell, 1999: 3). In a similar vein, Stuart Hall (1994) talks about the constructed nature of cultural identities. Shaped through differences and discontinuities, cultural identities are not eternally fixed in some essentialized past, but subject to the continuous play of history, culture, and power (Hall, 1994: 395). Always telling heartbreaking stories of discrimination, injustice, and violence, new political films generally have a gloomy atmosphere and a pessimistic tone. If there is still some room for hope and optimism in these films, it is because they acknowledge the performative nature of belonging and identity. New political films put emphasis on the process of 'becoming' that the characters experience. By the end of the stories, characters often come to open themselves up to new possibilities.

Taking issue with the discrimination against the Kurdish minority in contemporary Turkey, *Journey to the Sun*, for example, does not construct its story around a Kurdish character, but a Turk who is thought to be Kurdish because of his dark skin color. Instead of celebrating 'Kurdishness' as an oppressed minority identity, the film tells us about what it meant to look like a Kurd in Istanbul in the late 1990s. Discovering the poverty, destitution, and political oppression prevailing in southeastern Turkey, Mehmet Kara (ironically, the last name of the character means 'dark' in Turkish) is gradually transformed throughout his journey. Towards the end of his journey, Mehmet sits in a train compartment opposite a young soldier on military duty in the southeast. The soldier asks Mehmet where he is traveling to. 'Zorduç,' he replies, and asks the soldier where he is from. Responding that he is from Tire, the small town that is also Mehmet's hometown, the soldier asks whether Mehmet knows Tire. Mehmet replies: 'Yes. I had a friend from Tire. Mehmet, Mehmet Kara.' In this scene, as Kevin Robins and Asu Aksoy

(2000) suggest, Mehmet steps outside himself and assumes a new relation to identity: 'As he journeys to the sun, Mehmet crosses a border, and when he crosses that border – a symbolic border – he finds that he is then able to imagine possibilities that were never available to him before' (Robins and Aksoy, 2000: 218).

The female protagonist of *In Nowhere Land* also goes through a similar process of transformation. The film opens in a morgue, where the police show Şükran a body for identification whose face has been crushed beyond recognition. Not showing the body to the audience, the scene focuses on the woman's face contracting with pain. Fainting upon seeing the body, Şükran decidedly claims that she is sure that it does not belong to Veysel, her son. Towards the end of the film, several local men in Mardin who are connected to Kurdish guerillas tell Şükran that they will take her to see her son. After a trip through the mountainous landscape, she is brought to an empty village house where there is a young man waiting for her. Embracing him with great affection at first, Şükran soon realizes that he is not her son. The young man turns out to be a Kurdish guerilla called Veysel (Ruhi Sarı), a namesake of Şükran's son. He resentfully explains that he has risked his life to come to this meeting because he was told that his mother was looking for him. At first disappointed about not seeing their loved ones, Şükran and Veysel then get closer and share their feelings with each other. While Şükran tells him about her missing son, Veysel reveals that he has not seen his mother for years.

A few days later, Şükran is invited to the police department in Mardin to identify another body. The visual organization of this scene is almost identical to the morgue scene in the opening sequence. We first see the legs of one woman and two men, walking through a long and empty corridor. A door opens at the end of the corridor. A close-up shot on Şükran's face reveals the fear she can barely control. The white sheet covering the body is pulled off. Unlike in the opening sequence, this time the camera shows us the body. It belongs to Veysel, the Kurdish guerilla whom Şükran met at the empty village house. He was apparently captured and killed after that meeting. In a chilly tone of voice, one of the officers asks Şükran, referring to her missing son, 'Is this him?' Not fainting this time, Şükran replies in a calm, determined fashion: 'Yes, that's him, he is Veysel.' In the next scene, we see Şükran visiting Veysel's grave before returning to Istanbul. This sequence marks the transformation of the female character. Once a devoted mother preoccupied with the idea of protecting her son, now Şükran assumes the identity of the Kurdish guerilla's mother and seems to develop a different understanding of motherhood. While she once was opposed to the idea of relating her own experience to that of the Saturday Mothers, she now seems to empathize readily with them. Şükran's gesture of identifying the body of the Kurdish guerilla as Veysel is actually two-fold. On the one hand, she claims to be the mother of the young man and thus makes sure that he will not be buried anonymously. Visiting his tomb in Mardin, she does not leave Veysel, the namesake of her son, alone on his final journey. For Şükran, motherhood is now more than just a natural bond: it is about embracing the children of others as well. On the other hand, Şükran comes to admit with this gesture for the first time that her son might have been killed, just like the other Veysel. Performing the role of Veysel's mother is actually her way of saying farewell to her own son.

IV

With their thematic preoccupations, cinematic style, and mode of production, new political films challenge the notion of 'national cinema' and are closely related to the emerging genre of 'independent transnational cinema.' Recent debates in film studies have rendered national cinema a problematic category. The foundational problem of the concept of national cinema is its tendency to assume national identity as already fully formed and fixed in place (Higson, 2000). Also, it tends to take borders for granted and to assume that they are effective in containing political and economic developments, cultural practice, and identity. As such, a stable notion of national cinema cannot adequately account for the fundamental role played by globalization in much contemporary film production and reception (Higson, 2000: 67). Instead of taking national cinema as a fixed and uniform totality, a new reading of the concept that goes against the grain of its conventional understanding gains increasing prevalence in current film studies. Ella Shohat (2003), for example, indicates that the topos of a unitary nation often camouflages the possible contradictions among different sectors of society. She suggests that any definition of nationality in film studies 'must see nationality as partly discursive in nature, must take class, gender and sexuality into account, must allow for racial difference and cultural heterogeneity, and must be dynamic, seeing "the nation" as an evolving, imaginary construct rather than an originary essence' (Shohat, 2003: 57). In a similar vein, Susan Hayward points to the necessity of developing a renewed understanding of national cinemas in the context of processes of globalization that give rise to the multiplication of points of differentiation within and across nations (2000: 93).

Concurrent with the problematization of national cinema, a new genre designation has emerged in film studies, called 'independent transnational cinema,' 'accented cinema,' 'inter-cultural cinema,' or 'transnational cinema.' Hamid Naficy uses the term 'independent transnational cinema' to refer to an emergent genre that 'cuts across previously defined geographic, national, cultural, cinematic and metacinematic boundaries' (1996: 119). Independent transnational films made by deterritorialized directors share certain features that can be observed not only in their thematic preoccupations and formal aspects, but also in their processes of production and reception. In his 2001 book *An Accented Cinema: Exilic and Diasporic Filmmaking*, Naficy proposes the concept of 'accented cinema,' an

71

expanded reworking of his previous discussion of independent transnational cinema, to describe the films that exilic, diasporic, and postcolonial/ethnic directors have made in the West since the 1960s. The 'accent' of this cinema primarily emanates from the experience of displacement of the filmmakers and their artisanal and/or collective modes of production. Reflecting upon the home and host societies and the deterritorialized conditions of the filmmakers, accented films are interstitial because they are created astride and in the interstices of social formations and cinematic practices (Naficy, 2001: 4–5). In her 2000 book *The Skin of the Film: Intercultural Cinema, Embodiment and the Senses*, Laura U. Marks uses the term 'intercultural cinema' to describe the work of those filmmakers who are cultural minorities living in the West, often recent immigrants from Asia, the Caribbean, the Middle East, Latin America, and Africa. Intercultural cinema, a movement coming from the new cultural formations of Western metropolitan centers, emerges as a new genre characterized by experimental styles that attempt to represent the experience of living between two or more cultural regimes of knowledge, or living as a minority in the majority white, Euro-American West (Marks, 2000: 3). Drawing upon the theories of Gilles Deleuze and Henri Bergson, the particular focus of Marks' work is the ways in which diasporic filmmakers excavate and rediscover cultural memories through appeals to multi-sensory forms of recollection. Finally, Elizabeth Ezra and Terry Rowden define transnational cinema in such a way that it includes both Hollywood's domination of world film markets and the counter-hegemonic responses of filmmakers from former colonial and Third World countries (2006: 1). Taking transnational cinema not as a utopian discourse, they recognize the hybridity of new Hollywood cinema also within this category. In all these works, transnational cinema is conceived in a dialectical relationship with national cinema, instead of simply rejecting it.

New political films of Turkey have a close affinity to the emerging category of transnational cinema in terms of their mode of production. For one, all the films discussed in this chapter are international co-productions and/or include in the production crew professionals of various national origins. Aside from this international orientation, the way in which some of these films position themselves challenges existing national boundaries. *Mud*, for example, was promoted not as a Turkish film, but as the 'first film of a united Cyprus,' at the moment a non-existent political entity.[4] Although Derviş Zaim ranks among the leading directors of new wave Turkish cinema, *Mud* draws attention to his Cypriot identity. Similarly, *Waiting for the Clouds* is created in collaboration with Greek artists on several levels of its production: the story of the film is inspired by the Greek author Georgios Andreadis' influential story 'Tamama,' and Yeşim Ustaoğlu wrote the screenplay in collaboration with Petros Markaris.

What shows the affinity of new political films to independent transnational cinema is not just their mode of production, but also the political implications of their stories. These films problematize the question of national identity and belonging by directing attention to the multiplicity of the experiences of displacement, de-territorialization, and migration within the national formation itself. They call attention to the condition of being in exile in one's own homeland, community, and language. To adopt Ella Shohat's (2003) formulation, they do not so much reject 'nation' as interrogate its repression and limits. In doing so, they do not flee from contradiction, but install doubt and crisis at the very core of their stories (Shohat, 2003, 74).

Discussing *Journey to the Sun*, Kevin Robins and Asu Aksoy define it as a 'post-national' and 'counter-national' film in the sense that it is about 'releasing oneself from being a Turk' (2000: 218). For these authors, *Journey to the Sun* poses a question that national cinema can never pose: 'the question of change and the conditions of possibility of change' (Robins and Aksoy, 2000: 218). I think this observation holds true for other new political films as well. These films encourage the audience to conceive the past beyond the hegemonic discourse of nationalism. Moving away from an antagonistic understanding of history based on a divide between the notions of 'us versus them,' 'victory versus defeat,' 'our people versus the others,' these films open, in Ayşe Gül Altınay's terms, a 'space for critical thinking' that offers the audience new ways of facing the past without repudiating the shameful and agonizing episodes in it.[5] They create an opportunity to mourn for loss without falling into a nostalgic sense of innocence.

V

The main criticism that *Journey to the Sun* has faced in Turkey is that the film was made for a Western audience, not a Turkish one, and that it displayed an Orientalist vision. Addressing this criticism, Yeşim Ustaoğlu, the director of the film, talks about how her film has been received in eastern Anatolian cities. 'We went to Diyarbakır in the Southeast of Turkey,' she says,

> . . . in order to attend the opening of the film. The audience there was amazing. We saw the same situation in Van. The film was shown in Adıyaman and Urfa as well. I will never forget the reactions of the people there. They clapped for minutes and minutes . . . If the movie so emotionally engages people who live in more or less similar conditions and who deal with the problems seen in the story, how can you say this is a film for a Western audience? (quoted by Monceau, 2001: 30).

Ustaoğlu's comments bring to mind the question of 'whose Turkey?' If the audiences in Diyarbakır, Urfa, Adıyaman, and Van embrace the film, then who is the audience for whom the film was not made? Whose Turkey does the film not belong to? Obviously, the Kurdish audience's reception of *Journey to the Sun* was different from that of the mainstream Turkish media. This split reception holds true for other new political films as well. Challenging the long-held assumptions of hegemonic discourses, these films certainly pose unsettling questions about national belonging and identity.[6] In fact, they challenge the very notion of 'Turkish cinema' as a classificatory designation because of the emphasis on 'Turkishness' that it entails. The 'cinema of Turkey,' I believe, is a more fitting designation for these films, since it places the emphasis not so much on 'Turkishness' as ethnic identity, but on Turkey as a geopolitical entity and a locus of divergent ethnic, religious, and cultural identities.

3

THE CINEMA OF NURİ BİLGE CEYLAN

Arguably the most internationally acclaimed director of the new Turkish cinema, Nuri Bilge Ceylan is considered a contemporary *auteur* by many. Having spent his childhood during the 1960s in a small town near Çanakkale, a city in northwestern Turkey, Ceylan, despite his degree in engineering, pursued an artistic career, first as photographer, then as director. After producing the short film *Cocoon* (*Koza*) in 1995, he made his debut feature, *The Small Town* (*Kasaba*, 1997), two years later, at the age of 39. This was followed by *Clouds of May* (*Mayıs Sıkıntısı*, 1999), *Distant* (*Uzak*, 2002), and *Climates* (*İklimler*, 2006).[1] The films that Ceylan has made so far are characterized by a thematic and visual unity.

Adopting a small-scale and an artisanal mode of production, Ceylan produces his own films and enjoys having full control over all aspects of production. He prefers small crews. In *The Small Town*, for example, he worked with a crew of two, himself and a focus-puller. His crew increased to four for *Clouds of May*, and to five for *Distant*, including himself. In *Climates*, a more complicated project due to his use of the new HD technology and his own involvement in the film as an actor, he worked with a crew of fourteen. Trying to make his films look like photographs in terms of production style, Ceylan likes to remain solitary as much as possible during the shooting.[2]

With the exception of *Climates*, Ceylan has produced his own films and always earned enough money from television rights and awards for the production of his next project. As expected, he works with a rather small budget. *The Small Town*, for example, cost him only around US$50,000, and *Clouds of May* US$100,000. He takes several measures to cut down on the cost of his films; he shot the film *Distant* in his own apartment in Istanbul and used his own car as a prop. Working on a low budget is not only a matter of necessity, but a preference for Ceylan, who perceives 'minimalism' as his resistance to the culture of excess and the consumption craze characterizing the contemporary world (Ceylan 2003: 121).

Ceylan performs multiple functions in his films; these include writing, directing, filming, co-editing, and sometimes also acting. He prefers working with amateurs, for he believes that their acting is more natural. He often casts friends and family in his films. While filming, he does not show the script to the actors, but only gives them the details of the situation and explains what they should talk about. Contending that amateurs can imagine things that sometimes he himself cannot, he often decides the final make-up of the scene with the active involvement of the actors. We observe the same people appearing repeatedly in Ceylan's films. For example, his mother (Fatma Ceylan) takes part in each of his first five films from *Cocoon* to *Climates*. Muzaffer Özdemir, another regular in Ceylan's films, has played one of the leading roles in both *Clouds of May* and *Distant*. Özdemir also has a brief appearance at the beginning of *The Small Town* as the village idiot, a retarded man who the children make fun of. Mehmet Emin Toprak, Ceylan's cousin, played the leading role in *The Small Town*, *Clouds of May*, and *Distant*. Muzaffer Özdemir and Mehmet Emin Toprak actually shared the Best Actor Award in the 2003 Cannes Film Festival for their roles in *Distant*. Sadly, Mehmet Emin Toprak died in a road accident the day after *Distant* had been selected for the festival. Finally, Ebru Ceylan,

Nuri Bilge's wife, has had a small role in *Distant* and played the female lead in *Climates*. Apart from these amateurs, Nazan Kesal, a professional actress, has appeared in supporting roles in both *Distant* and *Climates*.

I

Ceylan's films offer a peculiar blend of documentary-style realism and highly aestheticized visuality. Depicting tiny details of everyday life, very little action happens in these films.

Cocoon is a twenty-minute black-and-white film without dialogue. It is about an old couple in their seventies (Fatma Ceylan and Mehmet Emin Ceylan) who live separately because of a painful experience in their past. The film describes a day they spend together in the hope of healing the pain of the past, although it does not turn out to achieve what they had expected.

The first three feature films that Ceylan made between 1997 and 2002 – *The Small Town*, *Clouds of May*, and *Distant* – can be said to constitute parts of a trilogy, since they seem to tell different temporal segments of the same story with the same characters. All three films revolve around the same trope: real and imagined journeys of homecoming, and escaping from home.

The Small Town constitutes an autobiographical 'homecoming' journey for Ceylan himself, since he returns to his hometown to make this film that reflects his own childhood memories. Written by Emine Ceylan, Nuri Bilge's sister, the film tells the story of three generations of a family living in Yenice, a provincial town near Çanakkale in northwestern Turkey. Shot in black and white, the film eloquently captures the rhythms of nature, the cycles of rural life, and the daily concerns of the townspeople. Roughly composed of three main parts, excluding the dream sequence at the end, the film opens with the images of a group of schoolchildren playing in the snow. After a series of stationary shots depicting scenes of the snowy town – empty streets, stray dogs, parked trucks, and the like – we see children reciting the national oath in the schoolyard. The rest of the first part takes place in the classroom of the poverty-stricken school. Inserted in this sequence are images of Saffet (Mehmet Emin Toprak), an unemployed young man, aimlessly drifting in the streets of the town. The second part depicts a brother and sister, Ali (Cihat Bütün) and Asiye (Havva Sağlam), returning home from school in the afternoon. On their way home, they wander over meadows and play with animals and trees. The third part depicts an evening that the entire family – Ali and Asiye's parents, grandparents, and their older cousin Saffet – spends on the farm. They eat and chat until the morning. The main source of tension in their conversation is the question of whether one should leave one's native town or not. Saffet wants to leave the town for a better life elsewhere, whereas his middle-aged uncle argues for the virtues of staying in one's hometown and making it a better place. The elderly grandfather tries to ease the tension by balancing these positions, while the grandmother becomes sad as she remembers her son, Saffet's father, who passed away at a young age. The children fall asleep as they listen to the adults' conversation.[3]

In *The Small Town*, *Clouds of May*, and *Distant*, one character – that is, Saffet/Yusuf, played by Mehmet Emin Toprak – occupies a central place in the narrative. In *The Small Town*, Saffet is portrayed as a young rebellious man who is desperately bored in his native town and yearns for a better life elsewhere.

In *Clouds of May*, Ceylan takes a further step into his self-reflexive exploration of the theme of homecoming and makes a film about the making of his previous film, *The Small Town*. The main character of *Clouds of May*, Muzaffer (Muzaffer Özdemir), is a young director, just like Ceylan himself, returning to his hometown to make a film about it. In the first part of the film, we see Muzaffer searching for locations and actors. He conducts interviews with the people of the town and undertakes some trial shots. He has a hard time convincing his reluctant parents (played by Ceylan's own parents) to play the elderly couple in the film. His father particularly is unwilling, not only because he finds the idea of acting awkward for a man of his age, but also because he is too concerned with saving the small forest he has cultivated near his property from confiscation by the authorities. Muzaffer's cousin Saffet (Mehmet Emin Toprak), on the other hand, willingly agrees to take part in the film, for he sees it as an opportunity to leave town and move to Istanbul with the help of Muzaffer. Although Muzaffer never genuinely invites him, Saffet perceives their kinship tie as a legitimate ground to move into his cousin's place.

The story of *Distant* depicts what would have happened, had Saffet's plans of moving to Istanbul come true. Here, almost the same characters are played by the same actors, but under different names. Set in a wintry Istanbul, the story depicts the morbid relationship between a commercial photographer, Mahmut (Muzaffer Özdemir), and his young cousin, Yusuf (Mehmet Emin Toprak), who has come from their native provincial town to Istanbul to start a new life. Yusuf comes to Istanbul in the hope of finding a job on a cargo ship; he thinks that such a job would provide him with an exciting lifestyle. Soon, however, he realizes that it is not easy to find a job, since an army of unemployed men are waiting for the same opportunity. As his stay in Mahmut's apartment drags on, the relationship between the two slowly begins to deteriorate.

Shot in HD digital video, *Climates* features Nuri Bilge Ceylan and his real-life wife Ebru Ceylan in the leading roles. The story tells of the prolonged break-up of a couple, İsa (Nuri Bilge Ceylan), a middle-aged university professor, and Bahar (Ebru Ceylan), his young girlfriend. The film is composed of three parts, each taking place in a different season and in a different city. The climates in the film symbolize the different moods in the couple's relationship. The film opens with the couple on vacation in Kaş, a tourist resort on the southern coast of

81

İsa (Nuri Bilge Ceylan) and Bahar (Ebru Ceylan) in *Climates*
(*İklimler*, Nuri Bilge Ceylan, 2006)

Turkey and famous for its archeological sites. On a hot summer day, we see İsa busy photographing the ancient ruins for a scholarly project, while Bahar accompanies him in a somewhat disheartened mood. The discord between the couple deepens further during a dinner at the house of a friend, and on the next day – which they spend on the beach. In the end, İsa proposes that they separate, and Bahar ends up returning to Istanbul alone. The second part is set in Istanbul during the rainy days of autumn. İsa runs into Serap (Nazan Kesal) with whom he has had an affair in the past. Although Serap is involved with another man, an old friend of İsa's, the two begin a relationship during which İsa learns from Serap that Bahar has left Istanbul to work as art director for a television series shot in Ağrı. The third part is set in Ağrı, an eastern town, in snowy winter. Tracking down Bahar in Ağrı, İsa proposes to rekindle their relationship. He asks Bahar to leave her job and return to Istanbul with him. He claims that he has changed and is now ready to get married and have children. At first Bahar rebuffs him. Then, at night she shows up in his hotel room, seeming to accept his proposal. The next morning, she wakes up in good spirits, happily telling him about the beautiful dream she has had. İsa, however, now seems to have totally withdrawn from his promises of the day before. He distantly asks her when she has to be on set, then offers to take her out for breakfast before his flight. The film ends with a shot showing Bahar on the set under heavy snow as a plane flies over her in the sky. *Climates* is set in three seasons: hot summer, rainy autumn, and snowy winter. The missing season in the film is included in the name of the female character, Bahar, which in Turkish means 'spring.'

II

Belonging is a major thematic preoccupation of Ceylan's cinema. Over and over, the themes of homecoming, leaving home, getting settled, and making commitments to relationships are evoked in his films. Always drawing upon an intrinsically unnerving aspect of home, Ceylan's cinema locates the source of the uncanny experience in the normalcy of everyday life. Home, with all its familiarity and intimacy, can be an engulfing place, a site of mundane acts of cruelty. The kind of malice that haunts home in Ceylan's cinema is not something that can be externalized or resolved; rather, it is inscribed in the very idea of belonging. Drawing on this engulfing aspect of home, Ceylan's films illustrate a sense of spatial entrapment with powerful visual symbols. In *The Small Town* the recurring image of an upturned turtle trapped by its own 'home' and in *Distant* the image of a mouse caught in a mouse-trap serve as symbols of a suffocating kind of belonging.

The trope of belonging is often connected to the question of provinciality.[4] The province signifies not a particular locality in these films, but a mode of feeling. It is about sensing that life is elsewhere. Literary critic Nurdan Gürbilek (1995) has suggested a particular feeling that can be described as 'the boredom of provincial life' prevailing in certain examples of Turkish literature. Referring to the experience of being left out, of constriction and confinement, the boredom of provincial life is not necessarily limited to the small town or the village, but it also may be experienced in the city. The province recognizes its provincial status only when it becomes aware of another mode of life that excludes itself. The province, in other words, perceives itself as provincial – that is, as lacking and deprived – only in relation to a center that marginalizes it. In this sense, the horizon of the province is always the big city, the center. Opening a horizon to the province, the big city also confines it beyond that horizon and fixes its identity as provincial (Gürbilek, 1995: 50–2).

What we observe in Ceylan's films, I believe, is a similar kind of boredom of provincial life. The center in the face of which the province recognizes its own provincial status is defined in two ways. First, the small town – a recurrent motif in Ceylan's cinema – represents provincial life in comparison to the cosmopolitan and sophisticated culture of Istanbul. Second, the small town itself becomes a metaphor for the perceived provinciality of Turkey as a whole in relation to the ('Western') world. 'Turkey is from the small town of the world,' Ceylan has stated in an interview. 'I started going to Europe when I was seventeen; the disparity of those places is startling. They also make you feel somehow the extent to which they view Turkey as the small town.'[5] Although this second meaning of the province is not always clearly articulated, I believe it is a subtle undercurrent in Ceylan's films. His characters, especially the educated and cultured ones, are aware deep down of Turkey's provincial status,[6] and their resentfulness is partly related to this perception. Ceylan's characters seem to carry an internal sense of provinciality wherever they go. The small town, in his films, is not something that one can leave behind. It would be more accurate to talk of 'the province within' in Ceylan's films, rather than of the province as a concrete space. His characters might

84

Saffet (Mehmet Emin Toprak) in *Clouds of May*
(*Mayıs Sıkıntısı*, Nuri Bilge Ceylan, 1999)

get out of the province, but they can never get the province out
of themselves.

Saffet, the character played by Mehmet Emin Toprak in *The
Small Town* and *Clouds of May*, seems to be the embodiment of
the boredom with provincial life. In *The Small Town*, Saffet is
portrayed as a young, rebellious man who feels entrapped by
his hometown. He desperately seeks to make people understand
that his entire life will be shaped by this place unless he leaves it
at once. Although the older family members want him to find
a job and settle down, he believes that he has no future in the
small town. In *Clouds of May*, Saffet appears as a young man who,
over the objection of his parents, quits his factory job to help
Muzaffer with his film. Failing the university entrance exam,
Saffet does not have any option other than finding a poorly
paid menial job, an idea that he strongly dislikes. His main
motivation for his involvment in Muzaffer's project is to find a
way to escape from the town. His dream is to go to Istanbul to
enjoy the opportunities of which life in the town deprives him,

or so he believes. The beauty of his town's landscape, which Muzaffer admires so much, does not make much sense to Saffet since he can only see an unchanging environment around him. The only time when Saffet has appreciated the beauty of his hometown, he explains in *The Small Town*, was the morning he left for his military service. It seems that one is capable of loving one's hometown only at the moment of leaving it.

Yusuf, the character played by Mehmet Emin Toprak in *Distant*, appears as a young man who has just arrived in Istanbul from his native town in the province in order to start a new life. The film opens with a long shot depicting Yusuf trekking through a snowy field to reach the main road from where he will catch a ride to Istanbul. In the background, there appears the small town he leaves behind. Yusuf comes to Istanbul to find a job on a cargo ship. Soon, however, he realizes that life in Istanbul is not as promising as he thinks. As his stay in Mahmut's apartment drags on, Mahmut makes him feel like an unwanted guest. Gradually, Yusuf is made to feel unwelcome not only by his host, but also by the city. Once a symbol of freedom and mobility, Istanbul gradually turns into a constraining space, not much different from the small town from which Yusuf escaped. Beneath its charm, the city is aloof and uninviting. As Yusuf's awkward attempts to communicate with others fail, he feels increasingly lonely and isolated.

The theme of provinciality is articulated in *Distant* not only in relation to Yusuf, but also to Mahmut, a character who supposedly is more intellectual and bourgeois.[7] At first sight, the story of the film is about the slowly deteriorating relationship between a guest and a host, as they both discover the many small elements dividing them day by day. A deeper look, however, proves that the morbid relationship between Yusuf and Mahmut arises not so much from the elements dividing them, but from what they share. What Mahmut sees in Yusuf is not simply a stranger with vulgar manners invading his private space, but someone who reminds him of something all too familiar and intimate. Yusuf's

Mahmut (Muzaffer Özdemir) in *Distant*
(*Uzak*, Nuri Bilge Ceylan, 2002)

provincial identity brings Mahmut face to face with his own
provincial background, the suppressed side of his own identity.
It is not Yusuf's alien presence that he cannot stand, but the
affinity between the two of them.

Distant is set at the intersection of two overlapping journeys.
While the direction of Yusuf's journey from the province to
Istanbul is the core narrative, there is another journey in the
film, away from Istanbul. During Yusuf's stay in Mahmut's
apartment, Mahmut's ex-wife is about to migrate to Canada with
her new partner. Mahmut feels increasingly disoriented by both
his ex-wife's approaching departure and Yusuf's unwelcome
arrival. Both journeys take place against his will and make him
feel more and more alienated from the life that he has established
for himself in Istanbul. 'Mahmut's house,' Ceylan has said, 'is
his prison.'[8] By the end of the film, he appears to be caught in
his own mousetrap. On the morning when his ex-wife leaves for
Canada, Mahmut finds out that Yusuf has also left. This double
abandonment marks the ending of the film. In the final scene,

we see Mahmut on the shore of the Bosphorus smoking the cheap local cigarettes that he once refused to smoke when Yusuf offered them to him. Ceylan considers this as a sign of hope, in the sense that the character is perhaps ready to change and that he has the potential to do so.[9]

While the idea of belonging, home, and hometown have a strong material presence in Ceylan's earlier films, it comes into view not as a major preoccupation in *Climates*, but as a strong undercurrent. In this film, belonging appears as a problem of commitment to a relationship and settling down. Time and again the idea of committing oneself to a relationship and getting settled is presented as a threatening prospect for men. İsa's mother, for example, pressures him to marry and to have children, while he obviously dislikes this kind of conversation. His colleague at the university constantly complains about his fiancée and the way she makes life difficult for him. One day, he happily declares that they have broken up, that he got rid of her before getting enslaved by marriage. Then, however, they get together again, because his girlfriend has grown more 'docile,' out of fear of losing him. When in Ağrı İsa tires of convincing Bahar to start over again, he claims that he has changed. 'I feel ready for everything,' he says, 'to get married, have children. There is nothing that I want for myself. I will succeed in making you happy.' These cliché sentences disclose that he perceives settling down as self-sacrifice, a kind of ordeal that he has to go through. In all these examples, making a commitment to a relationship is presented as a compromise on the man's part, since it is assumed that men give up their much-cherished independence when they settle down. Talking to his colleague about his winter-break plans, İsa tells him that he wants to go to a warm and far-away place. When his friend says that he would get bored by himself, he replies that for years he has dreamt of being alone. Yet, it seems, loneliness does not make him happy either. Just like Mahmut in *Distant*, İsa is a character full of bitterness, for no obvious reason.

While *Climates* explores the inner world of men, the woman is inscribed in the film as an absence. Spring, the woman's name, after all, is the only missing season in the film. Not showing that season, the film implies that spring is the season of making a commitment to life and to others, something that the male protagonist decidedly avoids. Although the entire story is narrated from the male protagonist's point of view, several small segments give us a glimpse of the female character's inner world. The film opens and closes with sequences of Bahar alone. Each includes close-ups of her face, which give us a sense of her agony over a relationship that inexplicably goes wrong. Apart from the opening and the closing shots focusing on the female character, the film also includes two dream sequences: the first is shown from the perspective of the female character; the second is narrated by her. During the hot summer day that the couple spend on the beach in Kaş, Bahar's dream (or rather nightmare) about being buried alive is represented as though it really happens. Coming out of the sea, İsa approaches Bahar, who lies sunbathing. He kisses her lips and whispers, 'I love you,' into her ear. He then playfully begins to cover her body with sand. Bahar smiles as her body slowly disappears. Then İsa collapses a large heap of sand onto her face, burying her head underneath. Waking up in a sweat, Bahar anxiously looks around. Reading a book next to her, İsa uncaringly warns her that it is dangerous to fall asleep under the sun. We hear about Bahar's second dream from her own lips, on the morning when she wakes up in İsa's hotel room in Ağrı. Apparently happy about their reunion, Bahar tells İsa that she has had a beautiful dream. 'It was a beautiful day,' she says, 'perfect sunshine . . . There were these rolling green meadows. And I could fly.' She softly narrates how she was gently gliding over the meadows, how she saw down on the hills her mother waving to her, and how happily surprised she felt thinking that her mother was still alive.

The first dream seems to convey Bahar's disappointment about a loveless relationship in which she does not feel valued.

89

Getting stuck in such a relationship is likened to being buried alive. The second dream reflects Bahar's optimism about their future together. On the basis of İsa's previous words, she falsely assumes that he is now ready to make a commitment to their relationship. The two dreams have a diametrically opposed structure: while the first is about getting buried under the earth, the second is about flying in the sky. The first one renders the woman immobile and impotent, the second makes her mobile and empowered. The first is about captivity, the second about freedom. Bahar is isolated in the first one, but spiritually connected with others (her deceased mother) in the second. Bahar's dreams reveal that freedom, empowerment, and commitment are not necessarily mutually exclusive values for her, while they obviously are for İsa. Spring is the season, it seems, that the male character will never know.

III

Ceylan has often mentioned that the artist who has influenced him most is the Russian playwright Anton Chekhov, especially in terms of the peculiar blend of humor and tragedy in his films. 'I think humor is always the brother of tragedy or sad things,' says Ceylan, 'and I think that with humor tragedy becomes more convincing.'[10] Here it should be noted that *Clouds of May* is a film dedicated to Chekhov. Among filmmakers, Ceylan cites Ingmar Bergman, Andrei Tarkovski, Robert Bresson, Yasujiro Ozu, and Abbas Kiarostami among his major sources of inspiration (Ceylan, 2003: 93). In fact, Ceylan's cinema is often compared to the cinema of the Iranian director Abbas Kiarostami because of his open-ended documentary-like style. Mentioning that Kiarostami is one of his favorite filmmakers, Ceylan goes on to say, 'with Kiarostami's films I really felt as if I was seeing my own country, Iran and Turkey are quite similar in appearance, at least in terms of the people and countryside.'[11] Just like Kiarostami's style, Ceylan's also relies on long takes and static shots. His films entail very few camera movements. Using minimum artificial lighting, he prefers to work with available light. Like Kiarostami's films, Ceylan's make use of long silences. What Ceylan's cinema also shares with Kiarostami's is a particular type of image that recalls Gilles Deleuze's vision of the 'time-image' cinema.

In his well-known argument, Deleuze (1989) talks about a shift from what he calls a 'movement-image' cinema to a 'time-image' cinema in Europe in the aftermath of World War II. Different from the movement-image cinema in which frames follow one another causally, as necessitated by the action, the time-image cinema is characterized by situations not necessarily extending into action. The time-image cinema, in this sense, frees time from causality. About the traces of the time-image cinema in Kiarostami's films, Laura Mulvey writes: 'This cinema of record, observation and delay tends to work with elongated shots, enabling the presence of time to appear on the screen' (2006: 129).

As opposed to the movement-image cinema where characters themselves react to situations, in the time-image cinema, Deleuze writes, 'the character or the viewer and the two together, become visionaries. The purely optical and sound situation gives rise to a seeing function, at once fantasy and report, criticism and compassion' (1989: 19). This visionary role of the character is all the more true for children. Speaking of the role of the child in Italian neo-realism, Deleuze contends that in the adult world the child is affected by a certain motor helplessness, 'but one which makes him all the more capable of seeing and hearing' (1989: 19). Kiarostami's characters are also visionaries, and the child's gaze plays a crucial role in his cinema. In a similar vein, Ceylan's characters are always visionaries. In his films, we often see the environment through the mediation of the characters. In *The Small Town*, the child's gaze dominates the film, and the children's keen sense of seeing and hearing is strongly emphasized. Ceylan's adult characters are also interested in seeing their environment rather than acting upon it. The characters played by Muzaffer Özdemir and Mehmet Emin Toprak in *The Small Town*, *Clouds of May*, and *Distant* are certainly of this kind. 'A new type of actor was needed,' writes Deleuze, 'not simply the non-professional actors that neo-realism had revived at the beginning, but what might be called professional non-actors, or, better, "actor-mediums," capable of seeing and showing rather than acting, and either remaining dumb or undertaking some never-ending conversation, rather than of replaying or following a dialogue' (1989: 20). Muzaffer Özdemir and Mehmet Emin Toprak function as 'actor-mediums' of exactly this kind. Having a peculiar withdrawn attitude, they mostly remain quiet and silently witness situations. A case in point is the scene showing Mahmut and Yusuf on a short business trip in *Distant*. Once having aspired to be an independent filmmaker, Mahmut now takes commercial photographs for a company producing floor tiles. He spends hours arranging lights and objects in order to produce perfect images of the lifeless, cold ceramic surfaces. Having taken thousands of such photos over the last few years, his idealism seems to have been totally eaten up by his professionalism. During their trip to a nearby town, Mahmut spots beautiful scenery with perfect light conditions. Sensing Mahmut's excitement, Yusuf suggests setting up the camera. After a moment of hesitation, Mahmut loses his motivation and simply drops the idea. Not even attempting to get out of the car, he rather watches the gradual disappearance of what might have been a beautiful image in front of his eyes.

Ceylan's characters are capable of seeing and showing, rather than acting. Through their vision, we become visionaries as well. Seeing the environment through the mediation of the character, however, is not the same as character identification. Ceylan blocks identification in his films by employing decidedly unsympathetic characters. It is interesting that his most unsympathetic characters are the ones who most closely resemble the director himself. The filmmaker in *Clouds of May*, the professional photographer in *Distant*, and the academic in *Climates* are characters that reflect Ceylan's self-image. What is more, in *Climates* Nuri Bilge Ceylan himself plays İsa, arguably the most unsympathetic of all of his characters, which adds a further self-reflexive ambiguity. Discussing new wave Iranian cinema and Kiarostami's role, Shohini Chaudhuri and Howard Finn (2003) indicate that Iranian films employ a similar strategy of blocking identification, through the presence of unsympathetic characters in the stories. 'This blocking of identification,' Chaudhuri and Finn argue, 'relates to the muted performances Iranian directors draw from their actors [. . .] a dedramatization that creates space for the intensification of images' (2003: 50). In Deleuzian terms, according to the authors, the failure of character identification breaks the sensory-motor chain and in a way liberates our senses so that we become more receptive to the optic and sound situations in the films (Chaudhuri and Finn, 2003: 51). The same holds true for Ceylan's films as well.

Ceylan's cinema pays close attention to the passing of time on the screen. As a filmmaker emphasizing time, Ceylan has a strong sense of the seasons, the weather, and daytime, which he explains as his own way of 'connecting things to a more cosmic state.'[12] *The Small Town*, in this regard, is a particularly interesting film because of its peculiar use of seasons and time of day. As I have discussed above, the film, apart from its closing sequence, is composed of three main parts. The first part, depicting the children in the school, takes place in the morning. The second part, showing Asiye and Ali wandering in the countryside, illustrates the afternoon hours. Finally, the third part, showing the night that the family spends together on the farm, covers the period between the early evening hours and the next morning. Describing sequential time, the story of the film appears to take place in a period of little more than twenty-four hours. In this way, the story might seem to present the cycle of a single day in a small town. This is not entirely true, however, because different parts are actually set in different seasons. The film opens in wintertime, with the images of children playing in the snow. The second and the third parts, on the other hand, are set in spring. Juxtaposing the cycle of a day with the cycle of seasons, *The Small Town* conveys not only the sense of monotony and boredom intrinsic to provincial life, but also the splendor of nature that colors it.

As its title indicates, *Climates* is also a film with a strong emphasis on the seasons and meteorology. Consisting of three segments, the film depicts a different season in each part: summer, autumn, and winter. The changing seasons in the film seem to reflect the changing moods of a relationship. The stories of *Clouds of May* and *Distant* take place over the course of a few weeks, and each film visually emphasizes the distinct characteristics of the season that it represents: springtime in *Clouds of May*, and winter in *Distant*.

The close attention that Ceylan pays to the seasons, the weather, and the daytime is manifested most clearly in landscape shots, which occupy an important place in his films. The landscape images in Ceylan's cinema are utterly beautiful in their plain, yet graceful delivery of nature.

Clouds of May ends with a sequence devoted to the depiction of the landscape that also recalls time-image cinema. By the end of the film, while the entire family returns back home after a night of filming in the small forest, Emin (Muzaffer's father) does not want to go with them. After everyone leaves, he spends some time alone in the meadows. He pours water on the ashes of last night's fire and collects the small garbage pieces they left behind. Then he gets an apple and sits down under a tree. Taking a single bite from his apple, he falls asleep. Meanwhile, the camera shows us the environment around him. The sun has not yet fully risen. There is an opaque light in the air. The brown-beige tones of the plain, the green silhouette of the nearby trees, and the pale blue of the sky above create a pastel color combination, the tones blending into each other. The forest in the background is still quite dark. The large tree trunks are noticeable only as dark shadows. Then, a pinkish light begins to emerge behind the hills. In the background, birds are chirping. Slowly we witness the light on the horizon becoming brighter and brighter, gradually lighting everything. Finally, the sun rises behind the hill. First, some dazzling beams of light appear; then an aggressive brightness invades the entire screen and turns it white. The film ends with this white screen. As we watch the whiteness, the bird sounds are still audible in the background. As opposed to the model of the movement-image where objects and settings have a functional reality strictly determined by the demands of the action, this sequence primarily constitutes an image and sound that is not extended directly into action. In other words, this is a situation 'invested by the senses' (Deleuze, 1989: 4). The camera makes us witness solely the passing of time. Ceasing to be derived from action, time appears as itself. It is time – in Deleuze's words, 'a little time in the pure state' (1989: xi) – that manifests itself on the screen.

Despite the predominance of lovely scenery in Ceylan's films, a sense of stasis and immobility is also intrinsic to his landscape shots, which at times produces an uncanny sensation. Anthony Vidler contends that the uncanny is a space-bound concept that finds its metaphorical home in architecture, 'First in the house, haunted or not, that pretends to afford the utmost security while opening itself to the secret intrusion of terror, and then in the city, where what was once walled and intimate, the confirmation of community [. . .] has been rendered strange by the spatial incursions of modernity' (1992: 119). In both cases, the 'uncanny' is not a property of the space itself, but a representation of a mental state of projection that elides the boundaries of the real and the unreal in order to provoke a disturbing ambiguity.

A case in point is Yusuf in *Distant*, whose relationship to Istanbul is based on seeing and watching from afar. Yusuf looks at the city from a spiritual distance in the sense that he cannot penetrate its surface, no matter how hard he tries. Reflecting Yusuf's subjective perception, *Distant* does not show typical urban images with busy districts and crowded streets, but quite peculiar renderings of the city, emphasizing solitariness and void. Caught in the rare white of a snowstorm, Istanbul appears barren and deserted in the film. In one scene, for example, as Yusuf walks by the docks, the camera follows him through the snow and comes upon a ship that is rusted, half-sunken, and tilted to one side. The ship stands there, in the words of one critic, like 'some relic of a forgotten civilization or a frozen mammoth.'[13] Eliding the boundaries between the real and the unreal, this image certainly produces a disturbing sense of ambiguity. Speaking of the representation of empty or deserted spaces in time-image cinema, Deleuze contends that characters wandering around these spaces are themselves emptied: '[T]hey are suffering less from the absence of another than from their absence from themselves' (1989: 9). Yusuf seems to be such an 'emptied' character. His condition in Istanbul seems to be more disappointing than his previous state in his native town, in the sense that he used to aspire to something back then. Yusuf realizes his dream by coming to Istanbul. There, however, he finds out that he carries an internal sense of boredom – 'the boredom of provincial life' – wherever he goes. Now there is no longer another place to go to. His dream has already been realized, without giving him what he had expected. He is emptied now, deprived not only of a fulfilling life, but also of the anticipation of it. Conveying a sense of inaction and stasis, there is something irreducibly uncanny in the representation of the urban space in *Distant*. Projecting Yusuf's mental state onto the space, everything in the city appears to be abandoned and frozen in time.

Ceylan's films, especially *The Small Town* and *Climates*, contain many close-up shots. These shots might focus on the faces of the characters, as well as on animals and objects. In both cases, close-ups appear to have an independent existence in the narrative, without having a functional reality determined by the demands of the situation. In *The Small Town*, there is a series of close-up and extreme close-up shots on the faces of the characters at the end of the film's third part, which describes the night that the entire family spends in the small forest. Revolving around trivial subjects at first, the conversation between the family members soon turns into an intense debate touching upon issues sensitive for everyone. Saffet's uncle talks about his own deceased brother, Saffet's father, as an 'interesting person who left this world without making any contribution to it.' The grandfather says that his son always escaped rather than felt that he was part of something. Getting upset by these negative comments about his own father, Saffet accuses his uncle of always speaking of his brother in negative terms. The uncle begins to recount the difficulties he faced in order to complete his education while his brother did not do anything to succeed in life. Remembering her deceased son, the grandmother silently begins to cry. Saffet resentfully asks why he should be the one who is always blamed for his father's troublesome life. He then turns his back on his uncle and closes his eyes, as though he wanted to show him that he ignores his words. After a while everyone falls silent.

Meanwhile, Ali pokes the fire's ashes to see whether there is any baked corn left. Seeing that there is none, he suggests his father goes and collects some more. His mind still preoccupied with the issues they have discussed, the father looks at him with empty eyes. Then, the faces of the characters appear in close-up shots from different angles; at times, the camera focuses on certain parts of their faces – such as the eyes, or the forehead – and shows them in prolonged extreme close-up shots. The series of close-ups in this sequence directs our attention to the articulation of the visual and discursive registers in the narrative. If we want to grasp an event, writes Deleuze, we must not pass along the event, but plunge into it, go through all the geographical layers that are its internal history (1989: 254–5).

The close-up shots in this section seem to create a similar effect of plunging into an event. At the beginning of the sequence, we witness the discord between family members mainly on the level of discourse. There is always something, however, that the words miss. This is something that one not only fails to convey to others, but also cannot fully grasp in oneself. The close-up shots at the end of the sequence make us realize the residue that cannot be fully captured by words. 'I think people lie all the time,' Ceylan has said in an interview. 'They never tell the truth. Underneath, there is always another reality, not available in dialogue. That's why I prefer to use gestures and expressions and situations; saying what the film is about with dialogue is not convincing for me.'[14] Close-up shots on the characters' faces function here to convey reality, something that cannot be achieved in dialogue. Ceylan's camera plunges into human faces to convey visually what cannot be captured in speech.

IV

A certain notion of 'play' is intrinsic to Ceylan's cinema. According to Donald W. Winnicott (1982), playing is an experience located in the potential space between the individual and the environment. There is continuity, Winnicott contends, between the play of children and the cultural experiences of the adults' world. Cultural experience begins with creative living, first manifested as play. Located in the indeterminable space between inner and outer world – that is, between the subjective reality and the world outside – playing teaches us to live with ambivalence arising from the blurring boundaries of these two spheres. Playing, in this sense, helps us to develop the ability to acknowledge the paradox without necessarily seeking to resolve it.

Ceylan's films, I believe, are more than anything about acknowledging the paradoxes of belonging. His characters ultimately learn to live with the paradox. Playing is articulated in these films at three levels: in relation to children and their play;

in relation to adults and their everyday activities; and in relation to the process of filmmaking itself.

As I have indicated above, child characters occupy an important place in *The Small Town* and *Clouds of May*. Both films decidedly avoid using the good old cliché of the innocence of childhood in relation to children's play. Playing retains a moral dimension for children, as much as it does for adults. It might take on different meanings, which at times include subversion, fraud, and even cruelty. In all cases, the experience of playing is closely linked to creativity. Through playing, children learn to test the boundaries of their inner world against the world outside.

The Small Town opens with the playing of schoolchildren who cause a retarded man to fall on the icy ground and then they laugh; the game entails a sort of childish cruelty. Next, we move to the schoolyard and see children in a row in front of a bust of Mustafa Kemal Atatürk, reciting the national oath: 'My duty is to love my youngers, respect my elders, love my country and nation more than myself [. . .] my ideal is to rise, to progress [. . .] I surrender my being to that of Turkey [. . .] happy is he who is a Turk.' After the oath, the teacher allows the children to enter the school building. The classroom, heated by an old primitive stove, appears to be in quite a deteriorated condition. After taking attendance, the teacher asks one of the students to read aloud a passage from the textbook. As the student reads the passage entitled 'Love and Loyalty within the Family' in an incomprehensible tone, we notice that the children do not pay much attention. The formal and prescribed language of the passage seems to make little sense to them. Accustomed to the boring hours they spend in school, the children apparently internalize the idea that education is something that does not touch life. Meanwhile, one of the students who has arrived late, probably because he had to walk a long way, hangs his wet stockings above the stove to dry them quickly; drops of water from the stockings fall on the hot surface of the stove. After a while, the voice of the student reading the passage fades away, as the sound of the drips is magnified. Now, the depressing mood in the classroom slowly evaporates with a game that the children instantly invent. They silently begin to play with a feather floating up and down in the air. As the feather begins to descend, one of the children blows at it to make it fly again. Then, a cat comes to the window, and the children's attention is directed to it. They begin to watch its playful gestures as it is tries to catch something, probably a fly, outside the window. The other sounds are now faded out in order to accentuate the cat. Identifying with the distracted attention of children, throughout the entire sequence the camera focuses on subjects unrelated to the lesson. We watch in long close-up shots the drops falling on the stove, the floating feather, and the cat outside the window. In the classroom sequence, playing becomes a subversive tool for students. They take the meaningless indoctrination of official ideology for granted. They mechanically repeat every morning the lines of the national oath commanding them to love their country more than themselves and to surrender their being to that of Turkey. They may not have the intellectual capacity to criticize what is imposed onto them; yet, it seems, they have an instinctual ability to undermine it.

Following the classroom sequence, Asiye and her younger brother Ali return home from school. Now it is springtime. On their way back home, the children wander around on the meadows. Everything they come across, from trees and animals to the gravestones in a cemetery, becomes an opportunity for play. Ali, for example, sees an old man sitting in front of his house. From afar, he throws a little pebble at the man, who keeps sitting motionless. The children watch their own reflection in a puddle. They see a stork making a nest on the top of an electricity pole. They idly spend some time in a cemetery, Ali tries to figure out the meaning of the Arabic inscriptions on the gravestones, Asiye eats plums from a tree. Hearing a voice from behind the trees, they become anxious, until Ali notices a donkey there. For a while, he examines the animal's face carefully, then he throws the plum stone at its face.

At one point during this idle afternoon, Asiye sees a turtle on the ground and begins to play with it. She explains to her brother that if a turtle is placed upside down, it will die since it cannot get on its feet again. Ali begins to play with the turtle, testing the strength of its shell by stepping on it. Asiye tells him not to hurt the animal. After a while, they walk away, but a few minutes later, Ali runs back and, after a moment of hesitation, places the turtle upside down. This little innocent malice, which seems to be a result of a momentary impulse of curiosity and cruelty, makes the child confront a border within himself as the image of the upside-down turtle returns that evening to haunt him in his dream.

Listening to the conversation of the adults during the evening that the family spends together, Ali falls asleep on his mother's knees. In his dream, he sees himself sleeping in his own bed. His mother steps into the room to cover him with a blanket, then goes to the window, in front of which some pigeons are perched. Next, there is a cut to the close-up image of an upside-down turtle desperately moving its legs. Then, Ali sees his mother again. This time she is on her knees performing *namaz*, the Islamic prayer ritual. He wakes up in his bed in a cold sweat and notices that his mother is lying in a strange position, reminiscent to the one she has taken in *namaz*, on the platform at the edge of the window. The woman appears to bend down, her arms over her head as though she wanted to cover herself up; the curved profile of the figure resembles that of a turtle. Getting scared, Ali begs his mother to get off the platform. The woman's body falls from the platform as though lifeless. The final image of the dream sequence is again that of an upside-down turtle desperately trying to move. In this dream, Ali probably discovers the boundaries drawn by his own conscious. No one has seen him tormenting the turtle, and no

101

one pronounces a verdict on him for what he has done. Yet, the sense of uneasiness arising from inflicting harm on another being leaves him disturbed. The figure of the turtle returns, displaced as the figure of the mother – the primal figure of belonging for the child.

In *Clouds of May*, playing is again presented as a transitional experience through which the child character negotiates his subjective world with outside reality. Ali, the grandchild of the family, also appears in this film, although he is now played by a different actor, Muhammed Zımbaoğlu. At the beginning of the film, Ali's aunt, Muzaffer's mother, gives him an uncooked egg and asks him to carry it in his pocket for forty days without breaking it. If he succeeds, she promises that she will persuade his father to buy him the musical wristwatch that he wants so much. The aunt's aim is to teach responsibility to the child. Taking this game very seriously, Ali begins to keep his right hand always in his pocket, holding the egg. On the day Muzaffer takes the child to the countryside for a test shooting, he softly makes fun of him, suggesting that, if he goes on like this, a chick will come out of his pocket. He proposes to find another way; for example, burying the egg somewhere in the garden every morning, taking it out in the evening, and pretending that he has carried it the entire day. Ali rejects this solution in naive honesty, suggesting that this would be fraud. Throughout the film, we witness Ali's sincere efforts to accomplish the duty assigned to him. One day, on his way home from school, he encounters an old woman asking him to take a basket of tomatoes to a house up on the hill. The child unwillingly accepts this request out of respect to an elderly person, and begins to climb the zigzagging path up the hill. When he bends over to pick up a tomato that has fallen out of the basket, Ali realizes that the egg in his pocket has broken. Pausing for a moment with a helpless expression on his face, he kicks the basket down the hill. The camera shows in slow motion from above the tomatoes rolling down. This image seems to mark a turning point for the child. Next, we see him running away after having stolen an egg from a chicken coop. The expression on his face is both anxious and joyous. He goes right away to his aunt's home. Muzaffer's father opens the door for him, saying that his aunt is not home. Ali waits in the living room as the old man types something in the other room. Out of boredom, the child beats the floor with his feet. The old man warns him from the other room not to make noise. Ali begins to walk around the room, looking at the photographs on the wall. He takes out a photograph stuck into the corner of a frame and examines it for a while. The photograph depicts his aunt as a young woman. Looking at the picture, closing first his left and then his right eye, he sees two different images. The camera identifies with the child's gaze and involves us in this play. When Ali is just about to put the photograph back into its place, his uncle, apparently getting distracted by the child's presence in his home, calls from the other room and tells him to leave and return later. These words seem to trigger something inside the child. He probably feels that he is being unjustly treated by adults. In an instant decision, he takes his aunt's picture with him instead of putting it back to its place. When outside, not knowing what to do with the photograph in his hand, he wedges it into a hole in the wall. At the end of the film, Ali's wish comes true, and even more: besides the musical wristwatch that his father buys for him, Sadık (Sadık İncesu), Muzaffer's assistant, gives him his musical cigarette-lighter as a gift. The play that his aunt initiated to teach him responsibility ends up teaching him something else: Ali has learnt that fraud is sometimes necessary in life. Muzaffer's initial teasing, it seems, has somehow gotten into him. In the night when his aunt declares the end of the egg test, he falls asleep in the small forest during the shooting of Muzaffer's film. In his dream, he sees himself wandering in the countryside. At one point, he takes his hand out of his pocket and realizes that there is a chick in his palm. He wakes up anxiously. The borders of inner and outer reality have become blurred once again.

In Ceylan's films, playing is an activity associated not only with children, but also with adults. Playing is part of the way in which adult characters arrange their environment, relations, and everyday life. In *Clouds of May*, for example, the obsessive efforts of Muzaffer's father to receive legal ownership of the small forest that he has cultivated close to his farm is not any different from the stubbornness of a child asking for a toy. Although everyone tries to convince him that his efforts are futile, the old man does not give up reading the laws and writing petitions to the authorities.

It is also possible to read the morbid relationship between Mahmut and Yusuf in *Distant* like an odd game of playing house. We observe the dynamics of a power game, not only in terms of the rules and limits that Mahmut imposes on Yusuf concerning the use of his apartment, but also in terms of the way in which Yusuf violates them whenever an opportunity arises. Getting upset by everything and anything – from the odor of Yusuf's old shoes to the crumbs of tobacco he leaves on the living room floor – Mahmut forbids Yusuf to use the main bathroom, to watch television or smoke in his apartment. As expected, these are the first things that Yusuf does as soon as Mahmut leaves. The same holds true for Mahmut as well. Despite the solemn posture that he assumes in Yusuf's presence, he returns to his true self whenever Yusuf is not around. One of the ironic examples of the odd play between the two is the scene showing Mahmut gravely watching Tarkovski's *Stalker*, a film that Yusuf, given his lack of an intellectual background, cannot possibly appreciate. In fact, he grows bored after a short while and goes to bed. The minute he is gone, Mahmut abandons Tarkovski and instead pops a porn video into the VCR.

Towards the end of the film, the odd play between the two takes a sinister shape with the introduction of two objects – or should we say toys? – that they use against each other: a battery-operated soldier and a silver watch. Having stayed at the hospital with his mother for a few days, Mahmut finds his apartment in terrible shape upon his return. Getting exceedingly annoyed, for the first time he confronts Yusuf, openly showing his discontent about Yusuf's prolonged stay in his place. 'One should be a little careful,' he says, 'in the place where one is a guest.' Leaving the room, Mahmut hears a strange noise behind him in the corridor. In a close-up shot, we see a small battery-operated soldier crawling towards him on the ground. At times, the soldier pauses to fire his little gun. Laughing loudly, Yusuf proudly asks: 'How do you like it?' He explains that he has purchased the toy for his little nephew. Getting even more upset now, Mahmut begins to question Yusuf. He asks what he is going to do if he cannot find a job. Is he going to return to the town? This is a sensitive issue for Yusuf, since he does not want to go back, no matter what. As a response, he switches on the little toy, which he now holds in his hand. The toy soldier fires his gun at Mahmut. Losing his temper altogether, Mahmut accuses Yusuf of being ignorant, provincial, and sponging off other people, and goes to the other room. Having been left alone, Yusuf once again turns on his little soldier. 'Turn that off,' Mahmut shouts from the other room. Meanwhile, he begins to search for something in the boxes and drawers there. An antique silver watch that he uses as an accessory in his photographs is missing. He asks Yusuf in an accusatory tone whether he has seen it somewhere. Embarrassed by this implied accusation, Yusuf desperately begins to explain that he has nothing to do with the missing watch. Meanwhile Mahmut spots the watch inside one of the boxes. He holds it for a minute in his hand without saying anything to Yusuf. Then, he quietly puts it back and closes the box. Meanwhile, Yusuf, unaware that Mahmut has already found the watch, keeps trying to prove his innocence. Although he is perfectly aware of the difficult position into which he has put his cousin, Mahmut leaves the issue unresolved. 'It doesn't matter,' he just says and closes the subject.

A cheap toy against a silver watch – two objects that Mahmut and Yusuf use against each other in their odd game of playing house. The battery-operated soldier becomes a symbol of Yusuf's provincial, supposedly vulgar identity. It symbolizes everything of which Mahmut accuses him. Not having the intellectual skills to argue against Mahmut's accusations, Yusuf turns his provinciality into a weapon against him. When he is at a loss of words, he lets the little soldier talk in his place. Mahmut, on the other hand, counters Yusuf's cheap, kitschy toy with a silver watch, not only an object with high material and cultural value, but, more significantly, a missing object. The missing watch proves to be a toy with more destructive power than a battery soldier. Yusuf's defense system collapses in the face of it. Now his provinciality is no longer a weapon, but something to be ashamed of.

Later that night, Mahmut and Yusuf are forced into an involuntary alliance by an altogether different cause. The mouse that Mahmut has long been trying to get rid of gets finally caught in the mousetrap. Waking from their sleep upon the strange noises of the mouse stuck to the glue-trap, Mahmut and Yusuf remain numb for a while, not knowing what to do with it. Mahmut suggests leaving the mouse in the trap until the morning, when the doorman would take care of it. Saying that he cannot stand hearing its sounds, Yusuf puts the mouse, along with the trap, in a plastic bag and takes it to the trashcans outside the building. He first leaves the bag next to the other bags. However, when he realizes that the street cats begin to approach, he does not want to leave the mouse to be eaten alive by the cats and kills it by hitting the bag several times against the wall. Even a simple act like getting rid of a mouse requires making a moral choice, whether to let it die in agony or put it out of its misery. Mahmut watches this entire scene from the window. This sequence represents another round in the two characters' game of playing house.

Moreover, playing is articulated in Ceylan's films in relation to the activity of filmmaking itself. As a film about the making of Ceylan's previous film, *Clouds of May* is obviously an interesting example of this. *Clouds of May* directs attention not only to the idea of play intrinsic to cinema, but also to the slippery ground between reality and fiction. In this instance, the playful dimension of cinema becomes most manifest in the performances of the amateur actors.

At the beginning of the film, Muzaffer with Saffet at his side searches for an old man, Pire Dayı (Uncle Pire, an elderly local man playing himself), who in the past used to dance at weddings. When they finally locate his small village house, they discover that the old man is in poor health. Nevertheless, he welcomes them warmly. Muzaffer explains that he is going to make a film and asks him to perform, as he did in the past. He adds that he is going to pay him. Indicating that he does not want any money, the old man says he will do whatever he can. Muzaffer wants him to repeat the lines after Saffet prompts them, as though he is speaking to someone. Having difficulties hearing, the old man tries to repeat the lines as best as he can. At intervals, he tells them about how much he misses his recently deceased wife, how difficult it is to live alone, and so forth. Not being satisfied with Pire Dayı's performance, Muzaffer and Saffet politely excuse themselves and leave. Back at home that evening, Muzaffer tries to convince his reluctant parents to play in his movie, saying that he cannot work with Pire Dayı since he asked for a lot of money. This little deception seems to work; upset at Pire Dayı's request for money, his parents finally agree to take part in Muzaffer's film.

By the end of the film, we discover that Muzaffer's father takes on the role that Pire Dayı rehearsed at the beginning. One afternoon, the entire family goes to the small forest for filming. The scene that they shoot is actually a segment of the final sequence of *The Small Town*, in which family members spend an evening together in the small forest cultivated by the father. During the shooting, Muzaffer is positioned behind the camera, while his assistant Sadık arranges lighting with a reflector and Saffet takes on the job of prompting from the script. The father is positioned in front of the camera, seated under a large tree.

107

After Muzaffer commands 'action,' the camera runs and the father repeats the lines prompted by Saffet: 'Well . . . / Here I am. / Now I earn my living as a farmer. / What difference does it make? / Nothing matters. / But, then, neither do I want to die. / If God allows, I want to live for at least another twenty years.' An external voice, the voice of Sadık, asks: 'Is it raining?' The father looks up and follows the lines prompted by Saffet again: 'What? / Is it raining? / I don't think so.' After the shooting, Muzaffer warns his father to be more careful and not to be late when he looks up to see whether it is raining. He complains that his father's acting is not good enough. The scene is repeated. This time, however, Muzaffer gets even more upset. He accuses his father of making long pauses between the lines. He reminds him that 10 million Turkish lira is wasted with each shooting. The father takes this warning quite seriously, since he is daunted by the amount of money being spent. He promises to be more careful. Muzaffer scolds others as well and warns Saffet not to make long pauses while prompting. After a small family squabble, they once again begin shooting. This time, however, Saffet reads the script so fast that the father cannot follow. Muzaffer yells at Saffet. The father gets upset about the loss of another 10 million lira. Muzaffer admonishes everyone once again to be more careful, and the scene is repeated. Everything seems to go right this time. The father completes his lines correctly. In the end, however, when the external voice asks, 'is it raining?' the father looks up and, instead of saying his lines, keeps looking up silently. Muzaffer loses his temper and starts yelling at his father: 'What happened this time, father? Why didn't you say your lines?' Still looking up at the tree, the father slowly stands up. When the camera shows where he is looking, it becomes clear that there is a red mark on the tree, indicating that it has been confiscated by the authorities. It turns out that during the day when the family was away for a trip to Çanakkale, the authorities came and marked the entire forest to be confiscated.

The ironic tone of this scene arises from the awkwardness of the situation that it depicts. Filmmaking, an activity usually associated with intellectual and artistic production, is transformed into a highly domesticated and humble practice here. An ordinary elderly man, who is preoccupied with concrete problems in real life, is made an actor in a movie by his son – a job that he perceives not only as an unnecessary disruption, but also as trivial and ridiculous for a man of his age. Irony also arises from the bizarre condition of 'playing oneself.' Muzaffer asks his father to be 'natural,' to be just like himself. This seemingly easy task, however, proves to be quite tricky, as the father seems to be incapable of giving a 'natural' performance as himself. Having said that, however, as we watch the scene we also know that the supposedly unsuccessful performance is already a successful one, because the father is actually giving a performance of failing to perform himself. This sequence reveals not only the playful side of cinema, but also the performative side of identity and belonging. Being oneself, it seems to suggest, is something performed, rather than something that comes naturally.

When we consider the examples above, Ceylan's cinema seems to take the experience of playing quite seriously. In his films, playing is always turned into a question of morality. Maybe this is where Ceylan's films most resemble Kiarostami's. Both filmmakers utilize the idea of playing in order to address existential issues – such as the meaning of life, morality, the conscious, and so forth – and in doing so they also draw upon the 'playful' nature of cinema itself. According to Hamid Dabashi (2001), what characterizes Kiarostami's cinema is simplicity, elegance, and matter-of-factness. His cinema demonstrates 'the unruly nature of life, the fact that living is good, that death is just there, and that life in its bizzare accidentality has a logic and rhetoric, a twisted irony, entirely of its own' (Dabashi, 2001: 69). For Dabashi, 'a different kind of morality,' actually a sort of 'countermorality,' emerges in Kiarostami's films, which is 'entirely contingent on the reality of the event itself and not on abstract ethical imperatives' (Dabashi, 2001: 55). It is possible to conceive Ceylan's cinema in similar terms. We can observe a similar simplicity, elegance, and matter-of-factness in Ceylan's films, which convey their story not through dramatic tension, but through details and nuances of everyday life. A similar sort of countermorality can also be observed in these films. Ceylan is never judgmental towards his characters; he never preaches what is right and what is wrong. Yet, he persistently shows that even the slightest move might have a moral dimension. Revealing the moral consequences of the small choices that his characters need to make in their daily lives, Ceylan's cinema playfully discloses that life in its 'bizarre accidentality' has a logic of its own.

V

There is something in Ceylan's films that persistently evokes the idea of 'home.' A series of different images in these films constantly takes us back home. The way that the old couple, played by Ceylan's own parents, watch television sitting side by side on a sofa, the father's old-fashioned flannel pajamas, the mother's hand-made extra-large vest, her never-ending complaints about her health problems and her insistent enquiries into her son's private life; the warmth and comfort of the house upon returning from the freezing cold outside; a piece of bread and cheese quickly eaten at the kitchen table; the dangling corner of an old, dirty curtain having come loose from the wall; a creaking window in the silence of the night; an upside-down turtle; a mouse caught in a trap . . . In these films, home means confinement and entrapment on the one hand, ease and comfort on the other. It is everything we wish to leave behind, and a place that we always long for. It is the province within us that we simultaneously escape from and return to. It is at once familiar, secluded, caring, boring, confining, and imprisoning. 'To leave or to stay,' Nurdan Gürbilek has written, 'this is the dilemma that home imposes – or should we say bestows – upon us' (1999: 75). Ceylan's films never seek to leave behind the tension arising from this dilemma. They never attempt to resolve the paradox of belonging; instead, they playfully acknowledge the paradox. This is where, I believe, the politics of Nuri Bilge Ceylan's cinema resides: it invites us to live with the paradox.

4

THE CINEMA OF ZEKİ DEMİRKUBUZ

Like Nuri Bilge Ceylan, Zeki Demirkubuz is also considered an *auteur*-director because of the peculiarity of his *oeuvre*. The seven feature films he has made so far – *Block C* (*C Blok*, 1994), *Innocence* (*Masumiyet*, 1997), *The Third Page* (*Üçüncü Sayfa*, 1999), *Fate* (*Yazgı*, 2001), *Confession* (*İtiraf*, 2001), *Waiting Room* (*Bekleme Odası*, 2003), and *Destiny* (*Kader*, 2006) – are characterized by a thematic and visual unity. Unlike Ceylan's open-ended style, Demirkubuz' cinema is based on tightly structured plots, sometimes with melodramatic overtones. His films revolve around either highly agitated or extremely detached characters. The prevailing mood in Demirkubuz' films is that of despair enveloped by a dark sense of irony. As opposed to the ordinary situations of everyday life depicted by Ceylan, Demirkubuz' films always draw upon highly dramatic and violent events, often involving murder and/or suicide.

Having had an unusual career path, Demirkubuz describes his initial involvement in film as 'purely coincidental.'[1] Unlike other new wave directors, who tend to have university degrees and a professional background in advertising and/or television drama, Demirkubuz is an autodidact who entered cinema with a secondary school qualification and acquired his university diploma while working in film. Born in 1964 in Isparta, a provincial town in southern Anatolia, Demirkubuz migrated to Istanbul. He earned his living working in menial jobs such as street-peddling. At the age of 17, after the military coup on 12 September 1980, he was convicted for his involvement in a leftist group and sentenced to prison for three years. Demirkubuz remembers his years in prison as a period when he began his education, since he spent most of his time there reading literature, most notably the Russian classics, and writing stories. He says: 'Sometimes I think that, if it wasn't for jail, I would not be a filmmaker.'[2] Once released from prison, he became involved in the film business by accident, rather than by desire. Having met Zeki Ökten in 1986, one of the prominent Turkish directors of the previous generation and an associate of Yılmaz Güney, he began to work in his films as production assistant. *Destiny*, Demirkubuz' 2006 film, was indeed dedicated to Zeki Ökten, whom Demirkubuz considers his master.

After working in the film industry as a production assistant for nine years, he submitted an entry to a screen-writing contest organized by the Ministry of Culture and received a credit award to make one of his stories into a film. In 1994, he shot *Block C*. The positive reception of his film encouraged him to make a second. Three years later, he made *Innocence*, which received several awards in national and international festivals and which most critics eventually recognized as one of the best films in Turkish film history. After the production of *The Third Page* in 1999, he made two further films in 2001, constituting the first two parts of his 'Tales of Darkness' trilogy: *Fate* and *Confession*. The third film of this trilogy is yet to be made.[3] In 2002, *Fate* and *Confession* were invited to the prestigious division of *un certain regard* of the Cannes Film Festival. In 2004, Demirkubuz made *Waiting Room*, a small personal film shot in his own apartment and with a small crew. Finally, he made *Destiny*, an epilogue to *Innocence*, in 2006, his largest and most expensive production ever.

Like Nuri Bilge Ceylan, Demirkubuz produces his own films; he owns his own production company – Mavi Film. With the exception of *Destiny*, he works within a relatively low budget, sometimes of around US$100,000, which he does not perceive as a problem. Similar to Ceylan, he performs several functions in his films. Apart from writing and directing all of his films, he has also taken up the tasks of cinematography and editing since 2001. While in his early films he often worked with professional actors, lately he too has begun to cast amateurs in the leading roles. Ufuk Bayraktar, for example, an amateur discovered by Demirkubuz, played one of the supporting roles in *Waiting Room* and the leading role in *Destiny*. In addition to the minor appearances he made in some of his films, Demirkubuz himself played the leading role in *Waiting Room*.

Demirkubuz has adopted a minimalist cinematic style based on straightforward continuity editing and few camera movements. Preferring medium and long shots, he usually maintains a distance between the subject and the camera. Lighting is often natural and understated. He does not like to use music in his films; when he does, he keeps it at a minimum and usually shows its on-screen source. As Chris Berry (2006) has remarked, the whole look of Demirkubuz' films is not just ordinary, but insists on being ordinary. It carefully avoids any softness, warmth, or otherwise aesthetically pleasing design that might give pleasure.

I

If Anton Chekhov is a major literary influence for Ceylan, for Demirkubuz it is another Russian, F.M. Dostoevsky. After reading *Crime and Punishment* in jail, Demirkubuz became obsessed with the Russian novelist. Talking about Dostoevsky, he has suggested that pain is the only thing that unites human beings: 'Pain is everywhere, we must all face it. All of my films are about it. Dostoevsky wrote the same book again and again with different characters working their pain through different situations. I try to make the same film over and over again.'⁴ Like Dostoevsky, Demirkubuz is very much concerned with the irrational side of the human psyche. His films are often about the characters' actions that do not have a comprehensible rational explanation: 'Things that are done for no evident reason constitute a no less fundamental side of human beings than things done for a reason.'⁵ Citing Nietszche, Demirkubuz contends that 'the human is as much an irrational being as he is a rational one.'⁶ His films, in this respect, present seemingly irrational behavior without necessarily justifying it through any possible social or psychological explanation. One such irrational act, desperate love that leads to destruction, is a major preoccupation of Demirkubuz' cinema.

Block C, the film that is Demirkubuz' least favorite, is about a middle-class woman living with her husband in a modern apartment complex in Istanbul. As her marriage slowly falls apart, she begins an affair with a young lower-class man who is already involved with the young maid of the house. Visually accentuating the high-rise blocks of the apartment complex, *Block C* shows the influence of the Polish director Krzysztof Kieslowski's television series *Decalog* (1988–89), which is set in a modern middle-class apartment complex in Warsaw during the socialist era (Demirkubuz, 2006: 6).

Innocence, Demirkubuz' break-through film, draws upon his favorite themes, desperate love and strange twists of fate. Including ironic references to Yeşilçam melodrama, the film tells the story of a young man, Yusuf (Güven Kıraç), who seeks to readjust to life after having served a ten-year sentence for killing his sister's lover – an honor crime. On his way to look up the father of an old prisonmate, Orhan, in order to get help to find a job in Istanbul, he stops in a town to visit his sister. There he becomes entangled with a strange couple who stay in the same cheap hotel. The woman, Uğur (Derya Alabora), is a bar singer, and the man, Bekir (Haluk Bilginer), a hanger-on, looking like her guard and pimp. The woman also has a mute six-year-old daughter living with them. Yusuf soon befriends Bekir and learns from him that he has been desperately in love with Uğur since their early youth, although the woman is in love with someone else, Zagor, whom we never see in the film except in a photograph. Apparently a hot-tempered man who cannot keep himself out of trouble, Zagor is transferred from prison to prison, and Uğur follows him from city to city. Despite knowing that his love is not reciprocated, Bekir cannot help devoting himself to Uğur. Observing this strange love triangle from outside, Yusuf slowly begins to get involved in the couple's life. One night, after another violent dispute with Uğur, Bekir commits suicide.

In the second part of the film, Yusuf has taken on Bekir's role in Uğur's life. Once a shy, introverted young man, he now adopts a roughneck attitude, similar to the one Bekir had in the past. He takes on the role of the involuntary pimp, although in fact he is deeply in love with Uğur. His love, however, just like Bekir's, is not reciprocated. At the end of the film, Zagor escapes from prison, and Uğur once again goes after him. As they are both killed by the police, Yusuf is left alone with the little daughter. When he takes the child to Istanbul to find Orhan's father, it turns out that Zagor is in fact Orhan, Zagor being his nickname. This strange twist of fate, however, remains unnoticed by the character, for it is revealed only to the audience.

In his most recent film, *Destiny*, Demirkubuz returns to *Innocence* and tells the story of the youth of Uğur (Vildan Atasever) and Bekir (Ufuk Bayraktar). The film is about the beginning of the desperate love triangle between Bekir, Uğur, and Zagor.

The Third Page, Demirkubuz' third film, takes its title from the types of news items that typically appear on the third page of Turkish daily newspapers, reporting violent domestic crimes. The film tells the story of İsa (Ruhi Sarı), a TV extra, who is beaten up and threatened by a gangster for US$50, which he is supposed to have stolen. Back in his basement apartment, İsa is about to commit suicide in desperation when his landlord shows up to demand back rent. Suffering a nervous breakdown, İsa follows the landlord to his apartment, shoots him dead and then passes out. When he wakes up, he is surprised to find himself back in his apartment. Taking İsa's testimony along with that of other tenants, the police cannot solve the case and do not charge anyone with the murder. Meanwhile, İsa befriends his next-door-neighbor, Meryem (Başak Köklükaya), a charming young woman living with her children and a husband who only occasionally comes home since he works in another city. Soon İsa falls in love with Meryem and cannot stand overhearing her screams at the hands of her abusive husband. One day, Meryem asks İsa to kill her husband. Upset by İsa's hesitant reaction, she implies that she knows he has already killed someone. When İsa forces her to tell what she knows, Meryem in a lengthy monologue confesses that she was the landlord's mistress for years, as the result of a tacit agreement between her husband and him. She was sexually exploited by both men. In the night when İsa shot the landlord, Meryem explains, she was in his apartment, saw what happened, and destroyed all the evidence implicating İsa. Later in the film, it turns out that Meryem actually had a secret lover, the landlord's son, and she manipulated İsa to get rid of her husband. The intricate story of *The Third Page* consists of many layers. The plot seems to echo the *film noir* genre with a *femme fatale* at its center and a deceived man who falls into a trap when trying to help this attractive and mysterious woman. This odd adoption of the *film noir* genre into an unlikely social context becomes further complicated by the religious overtones that the names of the main characters produce. İsa and Meryem are the Turkish names for Jesus Christ and the Virgin Mary. Among all his films, Demirkubuz has revealed, *The Third Page* is stylistically the most minimalist one, since it includes no music and camera movements (Demirkubuz, 2006: 12–13).

Set in Ankara, the capital of Turkey, *Confession* tells the story of a young middle-class couple who go through a painful process of separation because of the wife's infidelity. Harun (Taner Birsel), a successful and wealthy engineer, cannot confront his wife, Nilgün (Başak Köklükaya), after finding out that she is having an affair. Fearing that he will lose his wife, Harun wants her to confess the truth on her own, while she insists that there is nothing to explain. During a long night of fierce debate between the two, we come to learn that the couple's own relationship has actually been built on betrayal, since their relationship began while Nilgün was married to Harun's best friend, Taylan (a character we never see in the film except in a photograph, which actually belongs to the director himself). Although he never confronted the two, we learn that Taylan killed himself, probably because he knew everything. After their violent confrontation, Nilgün leaves home, and Harun pays a visit to Taylan's mother, who is not aware of the relationship between Harun and Nilgün, neither in the past, nor in the present. At first getting a warm reception, Harun is then asked to leave after he confesses everything. He goes through emotional turmoil, and returns home wanting to commit suicide, but then calls a friend to ask for help. Eventually, Harun recovers and accepts a job offer to go abroad. Before he leaves town, he learns from a friend that Nilgün has broken up with her married lover whose teenage daughter killed herself because of their relationship. Having lost her job and been rejected by her family, Nilgün now lives in a poor neighborhood on the outskirts of the city, expecting a baby. Harun pays a visit to Nilgün's less-than-modest squatter house and proposes that they get together again. After everything they have gone through, the two now seem to be in a sober mood and at peace with themselves. The film ends without revealing Nilgün's response.

Among all of Demirkubuz' films, *Fate* and *Waiting Room* are the ones that most directly address existentialist issues. Both revolve around emotionally detached and indifferent characters who display a cool suspicion of conventional truth claims.

Fate is a loose adaptation of Albert Camus' 1942 novel *The Outsider* (*L'Etranger*) to present-day Istanbul. Musa (Serdar Orçin), the main character of the film, is a clerk in a shipping office, living quietly with his elderly mother. Believing only in the essential meaninglessness of life, Musa lets everything take its own course without seeking any control over events. 'I don't mind' is the favorite expression of the character, and he uses it to respond to almost any question. His general attitude in life is to express his thoughts, when asked, as briefly and accurately as possible, without any pretense. In doing so, he inevitably defies conventional social expectations and established codes of behavior. For example, when one day he finds his mother dead, he does not show any sign of emotion and goes to work as if nothing happened. Later, when asked how he feels about his mother's death, he reveals that he is not saddened. He accepts the proposal of a female colleague, Sinem (Zeynep Tokuş), to marry, yet tells her that he does not love her, but finds her beautiful. He does not feel jealous when he finds out that she has a lover. When he is framed for a double murder, he again does not do anything, but accepts the course of events and goes to jail. Eventually he is released from prison upon the confession of the real murderer, his boss, who is also Sinem's secret lover. Not taking freedom as a cause for celebration, Musa quietly returns to his former life. Again, the names of the characters, as in *The Third Page*, produce religious overtones: Musa means Moses in Turkish.

Dedicated to the memory of Dostoevsky, *Waiting Room*, just like *Fate*, is marked by a subtle sense of dark humor and irony. Similar to Nuri Bilge Ceylan in *Climates*, Zeki Demirkubuz himself plays the leading role in this somewhat autobiographical film, next to Nurhayat Kavrak, his real-life wife; the film is set in the director's real-life apartment. The story is about a middle-aged film director, Ahmet (Zeki Demirkubuz), who tries to make a film adaptation of Dostoevsky's *Crime and Punishment*. Being in the habit of lying about almost everything without a reason – a habit that appears to be just the opposite of Musa's habit of always telling the truth in *Fate* – he falsely confirms the suspicions of his girlfriend that he is having an affair and does not care when she walks out. Then, he tells Elif (Nurhayat Kavrak), his young assistant, that he broke up with his girlfriend because she was cheating on him. Meanwhile, he considers casting a burglar, a young lower-class man who breaks into his apartment building, in the role of Raskolnikov in his film and begins rehearsals with him. Soon, he starts a relationship with Elif who, as her boyfriend discloses, has long admired Ahmet. Ahmet's indifferent attitude continues throughout this relationship as well. In the end, Elif cannot take it any more and leaves him. Ahmet, however, easily replaces her with another woman, this time a young actress who adores him too. The film ends by giving us a sense of this new relationship, which seems to be almost a replica of the former ones.

II

In Demirkubuz' cinema, home appears to be haunted by a routine malice. The houses that we see in his films, regardless of the social class of the characters, are always depicted as claustrophobic, confining places. Stripped of all of its romantic connotations, 'home' is represented in these films as a place of confinement, a prison that enslaves its inhabitants. The privacy of home does not make it a safe haven against the threats of the outside world. Home does not provide peace and quiet. On the contrary, its confined nature makes it a place where horrific forms of cruelty can be enacted without the intervention of others. A scene of physical and psychological acts of violence, home, in Demirkubuz' films, is where one feels most helpless.

In *Innocence*, *The Third Page*, and *Destiny*, home is directly associated with horror. As a film set in decaying hotel rooms,

Innocence presents a home only once. Close to the beginning of the film, Yusuf pays a visit to his sister's family home. He first stops by at his brother-in-law's workplace. From the conversation between the two, we gather that Yusuf's sister had run away with another man, Yusuf's best friend, while she was married. To cleanse the family's honor, Yusuf killed his friend and wounded his own sister. Since then, she has been mute. Feeling indebted to Yusuf for saving the family's honor, his brother-in-law, an aging man full of bitterness, welcomes him warmly and takes him home for dinner. At home, a poor basement apartment, his sister does not display any emotional reaction whatsoever to Yusuf's arrival. She quietly sets the table and serves dinner to the two men. As the brother-in-law drinks more, he begins to express his resentfulness more furiously, cursing his wife for turning his life into hell with her unbearable silence. Meanwhile, the eight-year-old son of the couple sits on the floor motionless, his eyes fixed on the television. The man complains that the same scene repeats itself every evening when he comes home. His wife goes to her bedroom, and the child watches television. Perceiving this attitude as a silent protest against himself, he continuously curses and shouts at his wife. At one point, he stands up, takes off his belt, goes to the other room, and begins to whip her. From the way in which this act is performed, we gather that this is a habitual night-time ritual for the family. Feeling uneasy with the scene that he witnesses, Yusuf takes his bag and leaves swiftly without saying a word.

In *The Third Page*, a similarly horrific scene is routinely acted out, also in a lower-class basement apartment. This time, instead of seeing it, we only hear it. At night, İsa overhears the screams of Meryem, who is brutally beaten and raped by her husband. Her home, which appears to be an ordinary place during daytime, turns into a house of horror at night.

In *Destiny*, we come across another version of these horror houses, this time in a building in a lower-middle-class neighborhood. In the first part of the film, we see Uğur as a charming young girl living with her family. She has a paralyzed father, a younger brother, and an attractive mother. Apparently having no income of their own after the father's illness, the family depends on the support of the mother's young lover, who spends most of his nights there. A strange sense of obscenity is in the air as the mother's lover every night visits first the husband's room to ask respectfully how he is doing and then enters the woman's bedroom to have sex with her. The very loud lovemaking is inescapably heard by everyone in the house, including the husband. While the young lover acts as a surrogate father figure to the family, he also seems to have an erotic interest in Uğur. The mother, being jealous, frequently makes violent scenes threatening and cursing the lover, although she knows well that she has no power over him.

Despite the strange and brutal events taking place in them, the houses in Demirkubuz' films look perfectly normal and ordinary. What is eerie about these houses is not so much the violence that openly happens in them, but the way in which it is normalized and rendered invisible. In *The Third Page*, for example, although horrific events take place in the apartment building in front of everyone's eyes, the tenants behave as if nothing happens. Neither the bruises on Meryem's face nor her screams seem to be noticed by anyone. Meryem tells İsa that on the night of the landlord's murder everyone was quietly watching television in their flats. The characters in Demirkubuz' films seem to be accustomed to violence, so much so that it is treated as a domestic affair. Horror does not come as a shock to anyone, since everyone knows it intimately. Talking about the details of her husband's planned murder, Meryem in *The Third Page* sounds like a resourceful housewife passing on a recipe. When İsa hesitates, she calmly says she would not mind doing the dirty part of the job herself, including slashing the man's face to make the body unidentifiable. In this sense, Demirkubuz' films show not only domestic violence, but also the domestication of violence.

123

We come across another instance of this domestication at the end of *Fate*. Although Musa's modest apartment is a relatively calm place, there is plenty of violence in the film. Apart from Musa's boss, who kills his wife and two children, apparently in a moment of fury, his next-door-neighbor Necati (Engin Günaydın), a young man living alone, is also a violent character. Visiting Musa one day, Necati asks for help in his plan to punish his unfaithful girlfriend. Telling Musa that he suspects there is someone else in his girlfriend's life, he is not fully satisfied by having her beaten up as a way of punishment. To get a more satisfying revenge, he now wants to invite her to his apartment, have sex with her and then throw her out, shouting into her face what a bitch she is. He requests Musa to write a letter – his own writing skills, he explains, are not very good – to bring her back to his apartment. This plan seems to work. One morning, when Musa and Sinem are having breakfast in Musa's flat, they hear the screams of a woman. They see Necati's girlfriend outside the flat, half-naked and with bruises on her face, having been thrown out. The two continuously swear and shout at each other. Later, the woman comes back with the police to have Necati arrested. Even later, one of the officers interrogating Musa about the murder case tells him that Necati is actually a pimp and his girlfriend probably a prostitute.

In the final sequence, when Musa returns home after having been released from prison, he finds Sinem living in his apartment with a small child; presumably Sinem gave birth to her lover's child while Musa was in prison. Seeming not to mind, Musa quietly sits in front of the television as Sinem makes coffee for him. Meanwhile, the doorbell rings, and Necati's girlfriend is standing at the door wearing a headscarf and modest clothing, in the manner of a traditional housewife. She wants to borrow an egg to cook scrambled eggs for Necati, whom we see in the background, walking around in his apartment in his pajamas. Regardless of their violent history, the two now have turned into a perfect domestic couple, acting out the roles of traditional husband and wife. Once again, violence is domesticated under the cover of normalcy.

The house is an uncanny figure in Demirkubuz' films in the sense that what appears to be most familiar and ordinary can quickly turn into unfamiliar and dreadful, and vice versa. In Anthony Vidler's terms, the 'uncanny' feeling arises from 'the transformation of something that once seemed homely into something decidedly not so, from the *heimlich*, that is, into the *unheimlich*' (1992: 6). Seeking to explain the feeling that arouses threat and horror, Sigmund Freud (2003 [first published 1919]) suggests that what we experience as 'uncanny,' as opposed to our common assumptions, is in reality nothing new or alien, but something that is familiar and old established in the mind, which has become alienated from it if only through the process of repression. Freud associates the ultimate experience of the uncanny with the most familiar place, the subject's former home: the womb, hence the figure of the mother.

What is striking in Demirkubuz' films is not just the extraordinary character of the malicious events, but the banality of the context in which they take place. The spaces in which horrific acts of violence are conducted are so ordinary that they all seem to resemble one another. What makes these films disturbing is the way in which horror is turned into something so banal and domesticated that it is no longer recognized as horror.

III

The imprisoning nature of home in Demirkubuz' cinema is accentuated by a strong sense of claustrophobia in the *mise-en-scène*. His films are mostly set in tight interiors. Events usually take place in gloomy apartments, dull offices, or decayed hotel rooms that are all alike. They are all dark, depressing spaces. The sense of claustrophobia is further strengthened by a framing technique that can be characterized as 'frame within a frame.' The action is often shot from behind an open door, a window, or a wall partially blocking the frame. As the action depicted in the image is shrunk in this way, the dark contours of the framing device function as a second frame within the frame, thus further intensifying the claustrophobic visual tone of the scenes.

Exterior scenes are quite rare in Demirkubuz' films. In those instances where urban space is shown, the signs demarcating the specificity of the space are effaced, to the extent that the city becomes unrecognizable as a particular locality. In *Innocence*, for example, most of the film is shot in İzmir, the third-largest city of Turkey, on the Aegean coast. Not showing conventional landmarks of the city, however, the film presents its location as an anonymous provincial town. Similarly, although *The Third Page* is set in Istanbul, it does not show any landmarks. Instead, most of the story takes place in the gloomy atmosphere of a basement apartment.

Prison is a recurring motif in Demirkubuz' cinema, not so much as a physical space, but as a metaphor for the way in which the characters perceive their own lives. Interestingly enough, when prison appears as an actual space in these films, it is stripped of its usual connotations, such as restriction and confinement. For example, the pre-credits sequence of *Innocence* opens in a prison, where we first see Yusuf as an inmate who has just completed his sentence. Seated on a chair in the prison governor's office on the eve of his release, Yusuf quietly listens to the governor reading loudly the petition that he himself has written. To the surprise of the governor, Yusuf declares in the petition that he does not want to be released, but to spend the rest of his life in prison. He explains that he neither has a job, nor any relatives who could support him. If the authorities do not allow him to continue to stay in the prison, he says, he will have to commit a crime so that he may return. Similarly, although in *Fate* Musa spends five years in prison for a crime that he did not commit, he never complains about it. Prison, it seems, is not necessarily a bad place for these characters; or they think that the outside world is not any different from prison. It is also interesting to note that, although the opening sequence of *Innocence* takes place in the actual space of the prison, it does not show any visual signs connoting imprisonment, such as bars or cells. When Yusuf steps into the outside world, however, he is repeatedly portrayed as being behind bars or within narrow and confined places.

Dominated by a claustrophobic visual atmosphere, Demirkubuz' films also generate a sense of confinement through the use of sound. The aural space of these films is often densely filled with disturbing background sounds that create a disruptive effect, most often that of a television set. For example, almost all the scenes in *The Third Page* are dominated by the presence of a loud and annoying background noise. In the opening sequence, as we see İsa being brutally beaten up by the leader of a gang, we hear in the background the loud voice of a sports announcer on television, narrating a soccer game. In the following scene, İsa goes to his workplace, a television studio, to find money. As he desperately tries to explain his situation to his rude and ignorant boss, we hear in the background the shooting of a television drama scene, a mafia killing. In the scene showing İsa and Meryem having a conversation at the breakfast table shortly after they have met, a loud debate in a daytime television talkshow goes on in the background. Later in the film, İsa cannot sleep at night because he overhears the violent arguments between Meryem and her husband. Even the quietest scenes of *The Third Page* often include the sound of television, dripping water, or traffic noise in the background. The main character's experience of entrapment is accentuated by the ubiquitous presence of meaningless and fragmented sounds surrounding him.

IV

The visual and aural regimes of Demirkubuz' films, therefore, generate a sense of confinement and claustrophobia. What further contributes to the uncanny nature of the spaces in these films is a pattern of compulsive repetition in the narrative. Demirkubuz' characters seem to be stuck in a labyrinth from which they cannot possibly escape. The narrative structure is always circular. There is no room for change, movement, or progress. In a confined world where there seems to be no way out, everything perpetually duplicates itself. All the relationships are the same; time and again, similar situations occur between different people. Even when the characters attempt to act differently, they always end up in the same vicious circle. No matter how hard they try, in the end everything remains the same.

The uncanny feeling in Demirkubuz' films, therefore, is not only conveyed by space, but also related to the idea of compulsive repetition. The recurrence of similar situations, things and events is indeed a feature of the uncanny. According to Freud (2003), a recurrent theme in dreams is the feeling of being lost in a forest or in the mist, with every endeavor returning the protagonist to the same spot. It is only the factor of unintended repetition in this experience, he contends, that transforms what would otherwise seem quite harmless into something uncanny and forces us to entertain the idea of the faithful and the inescapable, when we would normally speak only of chance. An involuntary return to the same situation might result in a feeling of helplessness, in the sense that it invokes the idea of something fateful or inescapable imposed upon the subject. The sense of compulsive repetition in all of Demirkubuz' films creates an abyssal structure that fosters an uncanny sensation.

We can observe this structure both in the circularity of the films' narratives and in the sense of compulsive repetition in them. In *Confession*, for example, the film has a circular narrative in the sense that it ends at the point where it begins. In the end, after the couple's painful break-up, Harun proposes to Nilgün that they start over again. Within this cyclical structure, the events in the story constantly recur to create a sense of excessiveness. The theme of betrayal, we learn, occurs for a second time in the relationship between the couple. The theme of suicide is also repeated three times in the film. Apart from Harun's unsuccessful suicide attempt in the middle of the story, we learn that Taylan, Nilgün's former husband and Harun's best friend, committed suicide, and the daughter of Nilgün's lover kills herself later in the film. In *Waiting Room*, we observe a similar circular structure: the film begins and ends with almost identical sequences. In both, we see Ahmet at night in a medium shot, working in front of his computer in his partially darkened room. Throughout the film, his relationships with women duplicate each other. In *Innocence*, the motif of muteness is repeated. There are two mute women in the film: Yusuf's sister and Uğur's daughter. Both are disabled because of male violence. In *The Third Page*, it is not just love affairs that are duplicated, but also murder plans. As İsa gradually becomes aware of the intricate affairs in his apartment building, he finds out that each adulterous relationship is a cover for another, and each murder plan is made to mask another.

The most interesting manifestation of the abyssal structure in Demirkubuz' films is in the connection between *Innocence* and *Destiny*. In *Innocence*, the narrative is circular at two levels. At one level, the story is composed of two circular parts. The love triangle between Bekir, Uğur, and Zagor in the first part is duplicated by the love triangle between Yusuf, Uğur, and Zagor in the second part. In the second part, we see Yusuf completely taking over Bekir's role in Uğur's life, not only in terms of his function as an involuntary pimp, but also in terms of his body language and posture. The same events are repeated in both parts. At another level, the entire narrative in *Innocence* comes full circle in the end when Yusuf, the main character, achieves his only goal: to find Orhan's father. Nevertheless, this is a bad time for the old man, since he is still mourning for his recently killed son. The film ends with Yusuf, along with Uğur's little daughter, quietly sitting in a room where Orhan's body rests under a white sheet, while the old man cries. With this ending, the narrative has completed the cycle. Disclosing that Orhan is the same person as Zagor – a photograph in his father's apartment depicts the same person as the photograph in Uğur's dressing room, a photograph that Yusuf never sees – the film reveals to the audience the identity of a man who had remained a mystery since the beginning. Surprisingly, Zagor, a figure whom we envision as troublemaker, turns out to be Yusuf's best friend, a quiet, peaceful man. The *mise-en-scène* employed in the final scene adds a self-reflexive dimension to the abyssal structure of the narrative. Having been the manager of a coffee-house in the Yeşilçam district in Beyoğlu, where the film production companies are located, Orhan's father lives in a building where film equipment is stored. The presence of these devices in the final scene calls attention not only to the fictionality of the strange turns and twists of fate in the story, but also to the constructedness of the text.

The abyssal structure of *Innocence* is deepened when considered in connection to *Destiny*. In the first part of *Innocence*, Bekir tells Yusuf his life story in a lengthy monologue sequence. From Bekir's story we learn that Uğur, Bekir, and Zagor are all from the same lower-middle-class neighborhood in Istanbul. Bekir is the son of a relatively well-off family. As a young man, he worked in his father's home textile and furniture store. One day, Uğur comes into the store, and he falls in love with her at first sight. He finds out that Uğur has a lover, Zagor, who is in prison. Bekir leaves Istanbul for his military service, and upon his return marries a traditional girl whom his family has chosen for him; shortly afterwards they have a child. One day, Uğur shows up at the store again; however, now she seems to have lost much of her dazzling energy. It turns out that Zagor has killed a police officer after escaping from prison. The police took both Zagor and Uğur into custody and beat them up in order to avenge the death of their fellow officer. Zagor has been sentenced to lifetime imprisonment. This is why Uğur comes to see Bekir, to ask for money for a lawyer. She says that she would do anything to help Zagor. After this incident, Bekir begins to follow Uğur, who goes after Zagor from city to city as he is transferred from prison to prison. Occasionally they break up, and he returns to Istanbul, but each time he realizes that he cannot live without Uğur and finds her again. During one of these break-ups, he learns that Uğur has married someone else and is now expecting a baby. For a while, she appears to forget about Zagor. When Zagor is transferred to another prison, however, she goes after him despite her pregnancy. Having learned about her involvement with another man, her husband brutally beats her up. This is the reason for her daughter being born mute. Discovering the cause of the child's handicap, Uğur stabs her husband and leaves him. After this point, Bekir leaves his family for good and begins to live with Uğur, moving with her from hotel room to hotel room. This is the story narrated by Bekir in a lengthy monologue sequence in *Innocence*. The same story also constitutes the entire plot of *Destiny:* In this sense, *Destiny* is a film that tells us what we already know. For the audience who

Musa (Serdar Orçin) and Sinem (Zeynep Tokuş) in
Fate (*Yazgı*, Zeki Demirkubuz, 2001)

131

has seen *Innocence*, *Destiny* is nothing but a repetition of the story in Bekir's monologue.[7]

The abyssal structure of Demirkubuz' films can also be observed in intertextual references to Yeşilçam cinema. Television is a crucial element of the *mise-en-scène* in Demirkubuz' cinema. Watching television seems to be the favorite activity of all of his characters, regardless of social class. One image repeatedly employed in the films is a shot of the characters watching television, taken from a point approximately where the television set is located. In other words, we see the characters from the television's point of view. *Fate*, for example, concludes with one such image: Musa and Sinem watching television. Even when the television is not shown, its voice is often still audible in the background.

One type of text that we often come across as background image or voice in Demirkubuz' films belongs to old Yeşilçam melodramas. Usually the voices we hear in the background are somehow related to the events in the story. For example, when Yusuf enters the hotel for the first time in *Innocence*, a female voice, apparently from a Yeşilçam film, says 'welcome' in the background. After Uğur follows Zagor, who has escaped from prison, Yusuf is taken into custody and beaten by the police. When he returns to the hotel in a terrible state the next morning, the cartoon character Casper asks in the background in an astonished voice: 'What happened to you?'

In the final sequence of *The Third Page*, İsa, after discovering by chance that Meryem's real lover was actually the landlord's son, follows her to her new apartment. He rings the bell. Seeing İsa at the door with a gun in his hand and asking for an explanation, Meryem stays calm and composed. Looking outside the window, she begins to recount the real course of events in a mechanical voice. She explains that everything she previously told him about her relationship with her husband and the landlord was true. The only thing she concealed, she claims, was her relationship with the landlord's son. She calmly adds: 'If you are going to shoot me, then shoot; if not, then leave.' Then she returns to the couch to watch television, as if İsa was not there. Throughout this conversation between the characters, we hear in the background the voices of a Yeşilçam melodrama playing on television. A weeping female voice asks: 'Why did you come here Oğuz? . . . why do you ask me to do this? . . . I have surrendered to my destiny . . .' A male voice replies: 'I have not surrendered my destiny, Ayşe.' The woman explains that she has done everything for her mother, to give her a comfortable life. 'You are lying, Ayşe,' the man says and claims that the woman herself also wanted a comfortable life – that is why she married a rich man. At the end of the sequence, İsa opens the door and leaves without saying a word. After he shuts the door, we hear a gunshot. Then, we begin to see the final credits of the film against a black backdrop. Meanwhile, we keep hearing the voices of the Yeşilçam melodrama in the background. The woman says: 'I loved you, Oğuz, I really loved you.' The man replies: 'Is this your last word, Ayşe?' These actually are the last words of the film. The connection between the film's narrative and the dialogue in the background is quite explicit. The male protagonist of the Yeşilçam melodrama seems to voice İsa's hidden feelings. Deceived and heartbroken, he blames the woman he loves for leaving him for money. Although the woman says that she left him for her mother – in Meryem's case, it is for her children – the man proclaims that it is the woman herself who actually desired a better life. In this way, the discourse of the Yeşilçam melodrama mirrors the story of the film.

The use of Yeşilçam melodrama in Demirkubuz' films produces a metafictional layer in the narrative. Patricia Waugh describes the term 'metafiction' as characteristic of a text which 'self-consciously and systematically draws attention to its status as an artifact in order to pose questions about the relationship between fiction and reality' (1984: 2). Revealing their own methods of construction, such texts not only examine the fundamental structures of narrative, but also explore the possible fictionality of the world outside. In this regard, metafictional texts 'tend to be constructed on the principle of a fundamental and sustained opposition: the construction of a fictional illusion and the laying bare of that illusion' (Waugh, 1984: 6). The use of Yeşilçam melodrama in *Innocence* and *The Third Page* seems to function as a metafictional layer in the narrative. While constructing a fictional illusion, these films at the same time call attention not only to their own constructed nature, but also to their close affinity with Yeşilçam melodrama. After all, the stories of Demirkubuz' films have melodramatic overtones in terms of the highly agitated and emotional condition of their characters, the role of chance and coincidence in the stories, the circular structure of the narrative, and the excessive use of certain themes and motifs – such as the theme of suicide in *Confession*, or that of muteness in *Innocence*. Revealing the constructed nature of their own fictional world, these films also point to the possible fictionality of the world outside.

The most interesting metafictional reference in Demirkubuz' films appears in *Destiny*, when Bekir learns that Uğur has left İzmir and comes to the hotel where she was staying in order to learn where she has gone. At the hotel, he finds the clerk watching television. Although we do not see the film playing on the television, from the voices we understand that it is *Innocence*. We hear the voices of the scene in which Uğur and Bekir have a fierce debate shortly before Bekir commits suicide. Pausing for a moment with his eyes fixed on the screen, Bekir asks the clerk what the movie is about. 'I am just looking,' the clerk answers indifferently. This scene can be read as a moment of flash-forward in the narrative, in the sense that Bekir sees on television a glimpse of his own future.

Metafictional references in Demirkubuz' cinema thus deepen the abyssal structure of the narrative and contribute to the sense of confinement and claustrophobia characterizing the fictional world of the films.

V

Demirkubuz' films, I would like to suggest, produce a tension that arises from the seemingly incommensurable thematic and stylistic elements that they incorporate. This tension is also what gives these films an ironic edge.

For one thing, there is an irreducible tension between the persistent idea of fate on the one hand, and the way in which characters are positioned in relation to it on the other. Fate is a theme that continuously recurs in Demirkubuz' films. It is symptomatic that the two concepts that are often used interchangeably, 'fate' and 'destiny,' are the names that the director has given to two of his films.[8] Similar to the films of Kieslowski, one of Demirkubuz' favorite directors, chance and coincidence play an important role in the lives of his characters. Fate appears in his films as a deterministic structure that overpowers individuals. Characters often seem to lead a life beyond their control. Unlike the rather cool characters of Kieslowski, Demirkubuz' characters are much more agitated and emotional. The director himself describes his characters as 'disempowered, entrapped and weak' individuals;[9] they are caught in situations without any way out. Stories revolve around journeys into entrapment in a social labyrinth where the characters are constantly on the move without going anywhere. What seems to be in contradiction to the portrayal of characters as disempowered, entrapped, and weak individuals, however, is the astonishing degree of self-awareness that they display concerning their own condition. Having surrendered themselves to their destiny – a presumably passive condition – characters nevertheless seem to make an active choice by accepting the predestined course of events in their lives. What appears to be a self-destructive attitude is often a self-conscious choice of the characters.

Monologue is a dominant narrative element in Demirkubuz' cinema. The self-conscious act of surrendering oneself to one's fate is often expressed through monologue sequences. In most of his films, the flow of events is interrupted at a certain point by a lengthy monologue through which characters explain their own position in relation to a certain important matter in their lives. These sequences usually represent a halt in the story, which momentarily immobilizes the narrative progress. The *mise-en-scène* employed in these scenes creates the impression that the confessing character does not necessarily address another character, but rather speaks to himself/herself. Monologue sequences in *Innocence*, *The Third Page*, *Confession*, and *Destiny* are examples of this. These sequences in which characters display a critical self-consciousness about themselves constitute an interesting connection between Demirkubuz' films and Dostoevsky's novels. The hero interests Dostoevsky, Mikhail Bakhtin writes, 'as a *particular point of view on the world and on oneself*, as the position enabling a person to interpret and evaluate his own self and his surrounding reality' (1984: 47). What is important to Dostoevsky is not how the hero appears in the world, 'but first and foremost how the world appears to his hero, and how the hero appears to himself' (Bakhtin, 1984: 47). What must be examined in Dostoevsky's novels, according to Bakhtin, is not the specific existence of the hero, nor his fixed image, but the sum total of his consciousness and self-consciousness, ultimately *'the hero's final word on himself and on his world'* (1984: 48).

In a similar vein, characters in Demirkubuz' films utter their 'final word' on themselves and on their world in monologue sequences. Bekir's lines, which are repeated in more or less the same way in both *Innocence* and *Destiny*, are symptomatic of the self-conscious choice to surrender oneself to one's destiny. These lines represent the character's final word on himself and his world. By the end of the monologue sequence in *Innocence*, Bekir remembers how he felt the day when he followed Uğur all the way to a town in eastern Anatolia: 'That night,' he says, 'I said to myself, my son Bekir, there is no way. It is useless to fight. This is your fate. Keep your head down and walk on this path quietly. From that day on, I walk on this path quietly.' In *Destiny*,

Meryem (Başak Köklükaya) in *The Third Page*
(*Üçüncü Sayfa*, Zeki Demirkubuz, 1999)

we see the episode that Bekir remembers in *Innocence*. Finding Uğur in Kars at the end of the film, he tells her how he feels:

> Everyone believes in something in this fucking life, and for me, it is you . . . I stopped at the door and thought. I said to myself, this is the door to the other world, this is the bridge between heaven and hell. Once you cross it, you cannot go back. Think twice. I thought and thought, but I couldn't go back. Then, I said to myself: there is no other way. Don't resist. This is your destiny. The road is set, bow your head, and walk.

Among the monologue scenes I have mentioned above, the one in *The Third Page* is somewhat different because of the cinematic style that it employs. Throughout the monologue scene, which lasts approximately six minutes, Meryem tells İsa about her terrible relationships with her husband and the landlord, both men abusing her. She is portrayed throughout the sequence in a series of medium and close-up shots narrating her story in a somewhat monotonous way, with her

137

eyes fixed at a point on the floor. Although she cries as she speaks, her tone of voice is distant and blank. Several times during the monologue, the unity between the voice and the image is interrupted: when Meryem stops talking, we keep hearing her voice over the image. Needless to say, such an interruption creates a disorienting effect on the audience. The use of sound in this scene can be considered in relation to Michel Chion's concept of 'acousmatic sound,' which he defines as a type of sound that is heard without its source or cause being seen (1999: 18). For the spectator, Chion writes, the filmic *acousmêtre* is off screen, outside the image and at the same time in the image. It brings disequilibrium and tension to the scene. 'It is as if the voice were wandering along the surface, at once inside and outside, seeking a place to settle' (Chion, 1999: 23). Although the use of sound in *The Third Page* is not exactly acousmatic – for its source is not outside the image – it creates a similar effect. The voice in the monologue scene seems to wander along the surface of the body, at once inside and outside. Just like acousmatic sound, it produces an effect of disequilibrium and tension.

In an interview, Demirkubuz has said that he used this strategy in this scene in order to convey that the character is actually lying.[10] Although she presents herself as a helpless victim, a passive object, according to the director, Meryem is in fact an active subject manipulating the events. This explanation, I believe, does not fully account for the effect of this scene. What Demirkubuz suggests may not be inaccurate, but somewhat incomplete. What Meryem tells in her monologue is at once truthful and false. It is true that she conceals her relationship with the landlord's son and tries to manipulate İsa to get rid of her husband. Yet, this does not rule out the fact that she has been abused by the men in her life. The fact that she makes murder plans does not mean that she is not a victim at the same time. Meryem is both an object and a subject in relation to the events in her life. Creating a distance between the voice and the body, the peculiar type of acousmatic sound employed in the monologue scene in *The Third Page* takes attention away from the content of what is being said to the externality of discourse itself. Speech does not naturally come out of the body, but it appears to have an alien presence occupying the body. In the case of Meryem's monologue, the question no longer concerns what she is saying, but how she is positioned in relation to the discourse to which she gives voice.[11]

The monologue scene in *The Third Page* is interesting also for the purpose of discerning another type of tension in Demirkubuz' films: the tension between realism and fictionality. Demirkubuz defines himself as a director who first and foremost pursues reality. This is an important characteristic of his cinema that he shares with Nuri Bilge Ceylan, who in an interview has said: 'I don't think my films [. . .] need to convey optimistic messages, I am just trying to be realistic' (Ceylan, 2004: 235). In a similar vein, Demirkubuz indicates that he is only interested in 'simple and naked reality as in the case of Dostoevsky's novels.'[12] Capturing 'simple and naked reality,' Demirkubuz' films nevertheless are also accounts of dense fictionality, which include intricate plots, repeating themes and motifs, metafictional references, and self-reflexive elements. Even a film like *The Third Page* – Demirkubuz' most minimalist film – might employ both dense fictionality and a self-reflexive stylistic device, calling attention to its own fictionality.

The tension arising from the simultaneous use of these seemingly contradictory thematic and stylistic elements makes Demirkubuz' films opaque, difficult to penetrate, and at the same time open to multiple readings. This is also where the ironic edge of these films comes to the surface. Writing about irony, Linda Hutcheon suggests that ironic meaning is simultaneously double (or multiple); therefore, we do not have to reject a literal meaning in order to get at what is called the 'ironic' meaning (1994: 60). The irony of Demirkubuz' films is indeed indistinguishable from their 'literal' meaning, and often it is impossible to discern whether there is actually any intended irony in these texts. For example, it is perfectly possible to read *Waiting Room* simultaneously as a film endorsing male chauvinism and as a film criticizing it. While at times it is more like a drama, at other times it appears to be dark comedy. The same holds true for *Fate*. The high drama in *Innocence*, *Confession*, and *Destiny* often makes us smile. Realism goes hand in hand with dense fictionality, which easily gives way to self-reflexivity. What is unique about these films is their stubborn opaqueness, which does not easily open up to anything.

5

NEW ISTANBUL FILMS

One interesting aspect of the new Turkish cinema is Istanbul's fading out of the screen. As indicated earlier, new wave films of the last decade tend to concentrate less on Istanbul and more on provincial towns. In those rather rare instances where the story is set in Istanbul, geographical, historical, and cultural characteristics of the city are usually erased from the screen to such an extent that Istanbul looks like an over-sized provincial town. This attitude is actually quite contrary to Istanbul's overall standing in Turkish cinema. The spectacular metropolis has always occupied a privileged position in Turkish film history. Because of the ubiquitous presence of the city in films, critics argue that Yeşilçam cinema could indeed be called 'cinema of Istanbul.'

According to İbrahim Altınsay, a Turkish film critic, a typical Yeşilçam film of the 1950s and the 1960s would begin with a view of Istanbul and establish its perspective as that of an insider to the city (1996: 74). Starting from the mid-1960s, social-realist films emerged in Turkish cinema. One of the most pressing social problems of this period was the growing rate of internal migration. Thousands of people from the provinces and rural areas were moving to Istanbul in the hope of starting a new life there. The films made in this period tend to reflect the experience of these newcomers (Altınsay, 1996: 74). A popular spot in these films is the historical Haydarpaşa train station, which represents a point of entry into the city. Many films made in this era begin at Haydarpaşa Station and present the perspective of someone who has just arrived in the city (Altınsay, 1996: 75). Identifying with the point of view of the newcomers, social-realist films sympathetically depict the new migrants' struggle to survive in a challenging environment.

In contrast to the privileged position of Istanbul in Turkish film history, the majority of new wave films seem to have lost interest in the city. This, however, does not mean that Istanbul has disappeared from the screen altogether. Instead, we can talk about the emergence of a new transnational genre of 'Istanbul films' in the last decade, a genre that offers alternative ways of seeing the city.

I

Somersault in the Coffin (*Tabutta Rövaşata*, 1996) can be considered a pioneering example of the emerging genre of 'new Istanbul films.' Director Derviş Zaim (2004: 46) describes the way in which he produced his directorial debut as 'guerilla mode of filmmaking,' in the sense that it was shot within three weeks under totally amateurish conditions and with 'no budget.'[1] Based on a true story, the film gives an account of life in Istanbul from the perspective of a homeless man who lives on the shore of the Bosphorus, receiving some small aid from the local fishermen. It presents two intertwined images of Istanbul: one is the Istanbul that the main character experiences as the physical environment; the other is Istanbul as a rising global city.

The first image of Istanbul is harsh and disturbing. Telling a story of exclusion, the mood of the film can best be described as agoraphobic.[2] Mahsun (Ahmet Uğurlu), the main character, is a vagabond who has no shelter from the freezing winter cold of Istanbul. This basic, yet vital problem of the character

142

Reis (Tuncel Kurtiz) and Mahsun (Ahmet Uğurlu) in
Somersault in the Coffin (*Tabutta Rövaşata*, Derviş Zaim, 1996)

constitutes the crux of the story. Living on the street, Mahsun
experiences the city as an agoraphobic space. His life is mostly
confined to a particular district, Rumeli Hisarı, located around
the Ottoman castle on the European shore of the Bosphorus.
One of the most picturesque spots of Istanbul, Rumeli Hisarı
has a beautiful view of the Bosphorus, complete with fishing
boats and ships passing by. Mahsun, however, unlike the visitors
populating the coffee-houses on the shore, does not perceive
the place as a view, but as a physical environment. The shots
depicting the beautiful scenery of the Bosphorus in the film are
always juxtaposed with close-up images of Mahsun's trembling
body, his hands and face turning black from the cold.

In *Somersault in the Coffin*, interior space is not depicted in
conventional terms. There is no conventional interior space

in the film that would constitute a counterpoint to the agoraphobic representation of the urban space. The film does not include even a single image of a house or any kind of domestic space. Instead, it produces the idea of interiority through unusual spaces. We can identify three different manifestations of interiority consistently recurring in the narrative.

The sole interior space in the film that gives a somewhat homely feeling to the character is the coffee-house where Mahsun occasionally spends his nights in exchange for cleaning the toilets. Interestingly enough, Mahsun experiences his most romantic moments in the filthy lavatory of the coffee-house, since it constitutes a private meeting place for him and the young woman with whom he is in love. A heroin addict, the young woman spends her days lonely in the coffee-house, constantly smoking cigarettes, her eyes fixed on the gorgeous view of the Bosphorus. She frequently goes to the lavatory to shoot up. In those moments, Mahsun has the chance for a brief conversation with her. The film contrasts the scenes emphasizing the cold and harshness of the outside with the scenes depicting the cozy and secluded atmosphere of the inside. While the boundlessness of the sea generates a sense of agoraphobia in exterior scenes, the warm, secluded atmosphere of the lavatory is presented as a sanctuary for the main character.

The second space that generates some sense of interiority in the film is the interior space of cars. Despite his shy and submissive appearance, Mahsun has a transgressive side to his personality: he is in the habit of stealing cars. He has the skill to break even into the most luxurious cars protected by high-security measures. His habit is to take cars for a joyride at night, and to return them to the same spot next morning. The vehicles that he steals are not limited to cars, but include trucks, buses, and even an ambulance. The car, Turkish literary critic Jale Parla contends, is a 'semi-private space,' for 'it is both inside and outside; it brings the individual into contact with the world at the same time that it shelters the individual from rooflessness, from perfect anonymity, or cold formality' (2003: 548). This semi-private status of the car is important for the character. For one thing, Mahsun makes use of cars as shelter. The first thing he does when he gets in a car is to turn on the heater. In the night when he steals a public bus, he takes it to a remote place and sleeps on the back seat until the morning. Apart from functioning as a shelter, the car also safeguards the character from 'perfect anonymity.' When Mahsun gets in a car, he becomes somebody. Taking the car in his control boosts his self-confidence and temporarily makes him an active agent. As opposed to the sense of stasis prevailing in the scenes shot on the shore of the Bosphorus, the scenes depicting Mahsun driving a car along the city's boulevards emphasize mobility and dynamism. We see Mahsun's face smiling slightly in these scenes, as the reflections of streetlights pass through the windshield.

The act of driving gives a sense of freedom and independence to the character. This is, however, a short-lived sensation since it always ends up in confinement. The scenes depicting Mahsun driving a car are always followed by the scene of him getting a violent beating at the police station. As opposed to the tranquil mood of the riding sequences, the scenes at the police station are composed of a fast-cut series of close-ups of Mahsun's bruised body parts as he is kicked and punched. The space of the police station constitutes the third manifestation of interior space in the film.

While the image of Istanbul that the character experiences as physical environment constitutes the center of *Somersault in the Coffin*, the image of Istanbul as rising global city occasionally surfaces in the background of the story. For example, towards the beginning of the film we see the shooting of a television program in front of the castle, in which a female journalist announces an exhibition. We learn from her words that Sultan Mehmet the Conqueror, after establishing the castle, decorated it with peacocks obtained from Iran. To commemorate this historical event, the current president presents fifty peacocks as a gift to be placed in the castle. Watching the shooting of the program in amazement, Mahsun attempts to get into the castle to see the peacocks. The official at the door, however, does not allow him to enter without a ticket. Although Mahsun insistently claims that the place used to be free of charge and open to everyone, he cannot get in. As he backs away in frustration, we see a group of Japanese tourists having their photo taken in front of the castle. In another scene, where Mahsun buys cheap wine from a snack bar, we hear in the background a radio news bulletin announcing that it has been decided to broadcast music in the Hagia Sophia in order to make the place more attractive for tourists,[3] but there has not yet been an agreement as to whether the music will be Christian or Islamic.

In these scenes, the image of Istanbul is that of a city eager to promote itself as a rising global center in the international arena, with its economic vitality, cultural diversity, and historical assets. According to Ayşe Öncü (1997), since the second half of the 1980s Istanbul has been rediscovered by its inhabitants (particularly the middle classes) from the viewpoint of the global. In the profusion of photogenic images, from advertisements to television, the aesthetics of the city's historical heritage have been seen anew through the tourist's gaze (Öncü, 1997: 56). Similarly, Çağlar Keyder suggests that Istanbul, rapidly becoming a city designed for cultural consumption during the 1990s, emerged as the 'showcase and gateway for Turkey's new era of integration into the world scene' (1999: 17). From the perspective of globalizing Istanbul, Mahsun is certainly a useless addition overcrowding the city. Systematically excluded from everywhere, he is treated as an alien element that needs to be kept out of sight. He cannot keep pace with the transformation of the city that he belongs to.

Peacocks become an obsession for Mahsun after his visit to the castle. He begins to enter the castle secretly by jumping over the wall just to stroke the peacocks. Mahsun is eventually ostracized by the community of local fishermen after crashing a

Mahsun (Ahmet Uğurlu) in *Somersault in the Coffin*
(*Tabutta Rövaşata*, Derviş Zaim, 1996)

boat he took without permission when trying to help the woman he loves to get over a heroin crisis. Cut off from everyone who supports him, he ends up roasting a peacock in the castle to save himself from starvation.

We can describe the main character's relation to the city in *Somersault in the Coffin* as a condition of 'confinement to open space.' Istanbul turns into an agoraphobic space in the film. Experiencing the city as a vast exterior space, the character hopelessly struggles to get in, to find a shelter, to be included. His efforts are doomed to fail, however, as he repeatedly experiences rejection and exclusion. Paradoxically, Mahsun cannot possibly get out of the city that he cannot get into. Stealing cars does not mean a flight to freedom for him; going away always ends in a return to the same spot. Movement is

147

circular and always ends in an aggravated condition of captivity at the police station. Thus, Istanbul turns into a paradoxical space that the character can neither enter nor exit. The film presents situations where parameters of space and movement never converge. Stealing cars, a transgressive act ostensibly suggesting a possibility of movement, does not get the character out of the condition of confinement to open space. The title of the film indeed accentuates this impossible convergence of space and movement: a movement requiring extraordinary skill, power, and energy on the one hand, and a space imposing stasis and death on the other.

Somersault in the Coffin presents an image of Istanbul very dissimilar to the previous representations of the city in Turkish film. The film takes the all-too-familiar image of the Bosphorus (an image that the Turkish audience knows intimately from its excessive use in Yeşilçam films) and turns it into something disturbing and alien. The Bosphorus shore, a district that traditionally connotes splendor, harmony, and happiness in Turkish cinema, turns into an agoraphobic space. Rendering the most cherished view of Istanbul uncanny and disturbing, the film makes us see the transformation of the city through a new lens.

II

The locus of new wave cinema has mostly remained limited to provincial towns in the decade following the production of *Somersault in the Coffin* in 1996. During the mid-2000s, however, a new wave of Istanbul films began to appear on screen. One of the most interesting examples of these films is *Istanbul Tales* (*Anlat Istanbul*, 2005), a film directed by five different directors: Ümit Ünal, Kudret Sabancı, Selim Demirdelen, Yücel Yolcu, and Ömür Atay. *Istanbul Tales* is remarkable especially for its innovative narrative style.

Telling five different yet overlapping stories about the intersecting lives of characters from different backgrounds,

Istanbul Tales adapts well-known fairytales – such as Little Red Riding Hood, Sleeping Beauty, Cinderella, Snow White, and the Pied Piper – into modern-day Istanbul. A gypsy clarinetist, Hilmi (Altan Erkekli), turns into the Pied Piper after finding out about the infidelity of his young wife. A transvestite call-girl, Banu (Yelda Reynaud), transforms into Cinderella when a young man working in a cheap Beyoğlu boutique falls in love with her without knowing her sexual identity. The innocent daughter of a mafia godfather, İdil (Azra Akın), turns into Snow White when she runs into a female dwarf in an underground construction site in Beyoğlu. The dwarf, who helps İdil to escape from her 'hunter,' the lover of her vicious stepmother, is the eighth and the only female child of a family of dwarfs; she has become homeless after having been thrown out by her cruel brothers. A schizophrenic young woman, Saliha (Nilgün Yeşilçay), the heir of a once wealthy aristocratic family, who now endures an isolated life in a Bosphorus mansion, turns into Sleeping Beauty when a young Kurdish man, a newcomer to Istanbul, breaks into the mansion. The young man, who can only speak Kurdish, turns into Prince Charming when Saliha takes him to be the ghost of her beloved great-grandfather. Finally, a Turkish-German woman, Melek (İdil Üner), who has just been released from prison becomes Little Red Riding Hood when waiting for her flight to Germany at Istanbul's new international airport. A popular journalist insistently tries to make her talk about the mafia involvement in the smuggling job for which she was imprisoned. She does not confess. As she moves to the gate, the camera reveals that the journalist himself actually works for the mafia – the wicked wolf disguised as the good guy. The parallel stories of these different characters are narrated in an overlapping fashion. The main character of one story appears as a supporting character in another. Voice-over narration is used in such a way that each story turns out to be narrated by a supporting character. The story of Little Red Riding Hood, for example, is told by her unborn child, a baby aborted six years ago, whose ghost has lived with its mother since then. The unborn child's narration is used as a framing device for the entire film as well.

The film includes a large number of characters, but the true protagonist of *Istanbul Tales* is actually the city of Istanbul. The film is shot in landmark locations: the Galata Bridge, Haydarpaşa Station, Eminönü Square, the backstreets of Beyoğlu, and so forth. *Istanbul Tales* makes use of a postmodern style of storytelling with its parallel stories, juxtaposed narrative elements, self-reflexive narrations, and different layers of meaning. Although each story is shot by a different director, there is visual continuity throughout the film, arising from the fact that all five directors worked with the same cinematographer.[4] On the whole, the film reflects a polished and aestheticized image of Istanbul.

Istanbul Tales foregrounds a decidedly mystical image of the city. Istanbul is represented as an enigmatic place with its peculiar geographical location, long history, and cosmopolitan culture. 'Istanbul is one of the most alluring cities in the world,' says the webpage of the film. 'Istanbul is a city of fairytales . . . Here, in Istanbul, even the most ordinary lives sparkle every now and then with fairytale magic.'[5] In this way, *Istanbul Tales* playfully draws upon a number of clichés circulating in Turkish popular culture as well as in the international media, such as the characterization of Istanbul as a place where East meets West. Despite its overall playful tone, the film itself seems to endorse an old cliché in the end – namely, the feminization of the image of Istanbul as a deceitful city. This cliché is often evoked in Yeşilçam films through the famous saying 'Istanbul, the slut' (*kahpe Istanbul*). It is usually uttered as an expression of the character's disappointment with the city.

Feride Çiçekoğlu (2007) demonstrates that in the history of Turkish cinema there is a long tradition of projecting anxieties arising from modernity and modern urban life onto the femininized image of the city. The figure of the prostitute is often evoked in Yeşilçam cinema to characterize the city.

Istanbul is imagined as an aging woman, still very beautiful yet promiscuous, who seduces men with her charms, only to destroy them in the end. The 'promiscuous' nature of Istanbul is often related to its long history and cosmopolitan culture. Istanbul, the capital of different civilizations from the Byzantine to the Ottoman Empire, has seen the rise and fall of great powers over the centuries; yet, the city itself has survived the devastating events of history. After the 1950s, a recurring theme in Turkish cinema is the story of provincial characters seduced by Istanbul.[6] The 'deceitful' nature of the city in these films is always associated with the presence of independent, modern women on its streets. Connoting availability, these women are regarded as potential prostitutes. They become both a major attraction and a potential threat for men. More often than not, these women bring destruction to men. In those cases where the film ends happily, the male protagonist 'rescues' the woman from the city and takes her back to where she 'naturally' belongs, the security of home and domesticity. As such, Istanbul is represented as a potential source of contamination and corruption. Anxieties arising from modernity and modern urban life are projected onto Istanbul through the figure of the modern independent woman perceived as a potential prostitute.

The final sequence of *Istanbul Tales* evokes this old cliché in Turkish cinema. The single event that connects all five stories in the film is the killing of a famous mafia leader, the father of Snow White. The development of each story is somehow triggered by this event throughout the course of approximately twenty-four hours. At the dawn of the following morning, the paths of several characters from the different stories intersect on the Galata Bridge. Having managed to run away from her 'hunter,' Snow White comes to the bridge with the eighth dwarf. Cinderella, disappointed by her 'prince,' who does not show up at midnight at the train station where they were supposed to meet in order to run away from Istanbul, spends the night sleeping on a chair in a coffee-house near the bridge. She is with

151

an aging gay friend who protects her from her violent pimp. The young Kurdish man who broke into Sleeping Beauty's mansion spends the night on a bench in a park near the bridge, since he has nowhere else to go. The gypsy clarinetist, finally, after having found his wife in bed with another man, walks the streets of the city the entire night and arrives at the bridge early in the morning. Not knowing one another, these different characters are brought together by the mesmerizing tune of the Pied Piper's music. The clarinetist starts an angry tirade on the bridge before playing his instrument. His resentful remarks are aimed at the city, which he holds responsible for all the bad things that ever happened to him. 'Istanbul is over,' he shouts, 'let's go find another place . . . I'll take everybody away . . . you will stay all alone, Istanbul, alone and deserted . . . wake up, Istanbul, the slut . . . we have been fooled by your fairy-tales and you destroyed our lives. . . wake up everybody, the fairy-tale is over.' The words of the clarinetist obviously resonate with the cliché of the deceitful city. Istanbul, in his tirade, is declared to be a slut who deceives people with false hopes and makes them miserable. The clarinetist hopes that the beautiful sound of his music will awake the people of Istanbul to the truth about their city. As he crosses the Galata Bridge, playing his instrument, the characters from the other stories begin to follow him, as though being mesmerized by his music. Being convinced that 'Istanbul is over,' they all seem to leave the city to find another place. It is interesting to note that the characters we see in the final sequence mostly represent subordinate identities in modern-day Istanbul: a transvestite prostitute, a gay man, a homeless handicapped woman, a gypsy musician, and an unemployed Kurdish man. The affluence and cosmopolitan culture of the city attracts these people with the promise of a better life. In Istanbul, however, they are stuck in an aggravated condition of poverty, corruption and oppression. The fairytale the city promises turns into a nightmare. Their only lasting hope now is to leave the city. Little Red Riding Hood, the Turkish-German woman, is the only absentee from this picture, as a character who holds a marginal identity. She is not among the characters seeking to escape from Istanbul, since she has already left the city for Germany. 'I don't want your corrupt Istanbul,' she says to a man just before her departure.

The innovative style of *Istanbul Tales* seems to come down in the end to a good old cliché. It is not quite clear to what extent the film playfully engages with this cliché and to what extent it uncritically reproduces it.

III

Another important film of the mid-2000s that puts Istanbul at center stage is Turkish-German director Fatih Akın's *Crossing the Bridge: The Sound of Istanbul* (*Istanbul Hatırası*, 2005), a documentary about different music scenes in Istanbul. *Crossing the Bridge* positions itself quite differently from *Istanbul Tales* in relation to the city. Instead of mystifying Istanbul, it rather materializes the city. Instead of suggesting a move away from Istanbul, it moves deep into the city. Instead of unmasking the 'truth' of the city, it suggests that there is no truth beyond the multiplicity of contradictory, yet interacting voices in it. Before discussing *Crossing the Bridge*, I will first briefly look at the image of Istanbul in Akın's previous film, *Head-On* (*Duvara Karşı/ Gegen die Wand*, 2004). Both German productions, neither *Head-On* nor *Crossing the Bridge* is part of new Turkish cinema.[7] Yet, the peculiar imagery of Istanbul in both films makes them rank among the major Istanbul films of the last decade. Akın himself affirms this observation, stating that the biggest compliment he received so far was that the Turkish film world saw *Head-On* as part of Turkish cinema.[8] Here, I will discuss *Head-On* and *Crossing the Bridge* as transnational Istanbul films by a Turkish-German director.

Winning the 2004 European Film Award and the Golden Bear award at the 2004 Berlinale, *Head-On* is a love story set in

two cities: Hamburg and Istanbul. The two main protagonists
of the film are members of the second generation of Turkish
immigrants in Germany, like Akın himself. At the beginning
of the story, we see Cahit (Birol Ünel), a drunken aging punk
rocker, driving his car at full speed into a wall. In the hospital,
he meets Sibel (Sibel Kekilli), an attractive young woman who
attempted to commit suicide because of her oppressive family.
They enter a sham marriage to get rid of Sibel's family. In the
first weeks of their life together, Sibel takes advantage of her
recently achieved freedom, dancing in clubs and sleeping with
men she likes. Despite the obvious attraction between the two,
she does not make love to Cahit, since she thinks that this
would ruin her much-cherished independence. These happy
days come to an end when Cahit one night unintentionally kills
a friend after he made insulting remarks about Sibel. Suddenly
there occurs a radical shift in the tone of the film. Cahit is
imprisoned. Sibel is devastated, for she finally recognizes how
much she has been in love with Cahit. Meanwhile, she realizes
that her brother might kill her to save the family honor. Before
fleeing to Istanbul to protect herself, she visits Cahit in prison
and tells him that she will wait for him. In Istanbul, we see a
different Sibel. She now seems to have lost all of her vibrant
energy. Working as a chambermaid at a hotel, she at first adopts
a strictly conservative lifestyle. After a while, however, she
turns to ruthless self-destruction, very much like Cahit's at the
beginning of the film. Now, it is Sibel's turn to run, as the film
title suggests, 'head-on into the wall' and crash. At the end of
the film, Cahit and Sibel finally get together in Istanbul after
Cahit is released from prison. It seems too late, however, for the
two to start over, since Sibel now has family of her own with a
little daughter.

Head-On is divided into two segments. The tone of the
segment set in Hamburg is rather playful and light-hearted,
whereas the segment set in Istanbul is darker and melancholic.
Apart from dominating the second part of the story, the image

of Istanbul is also used as a framing device in the narrative. *Head-On* begins and ends with a peculiar image of Istanbul that is also inserted several times between the events in the narrative. As the title of the film appears, we hear a male voice in the background counting 'one, two, three, four,' in Turkish, as though counting in a band at the beginning of a performance. Then, the film opens with a musical sequence. The first image is a medium-long shot of a band of six facing the camera. The musicians, dressed in black suits, are seated on a row of chairs; at the center there is a standing female singer in a red dress. The band is located on the shore of the Golden Horn, with a view of the silhouette of the old city across the water, complete with historical landmarks such as the Süleymaniye Mosque. The ground on which the band performs is covered by red carpets arranged asymmetrically on top of one another. 'The carpets,' Deniz Göktürk suggests, 'create a stage for the open-air performance of the ensemble and unsettle the opposition between indoor and outdoor, suggesting also a conflation of public and private spaces, a fusion between theatrical stages and "real" locations' (2008: 156). The singer performs a song that sounds like traditional Turkish music in a modest, somewhat old-fashion style, without any flashy gestures. Shot from a fixed, somewhat distant camera position, this image evokes the visual aura of an old postcard or a record-sleeve one would find in an antique shop in Istanbul. Both the image and the song seem to suggest an obscure temporality in the sense that they appear simultaneously familiar and intimate on the one hand, and distant and mysterious on the other. We see these musical sequences inserted into the narrative six times throughout the film. While the *mise-en-scène* remains the same, different songs are performed each time. Usually, we first begin hearing the music in the background, then the image appears. The film closes with a musical sequence in the same way in which it opens. Unlike the opening sequence, however, the musicians stand up and salute the audience at the end of their performance.

Akın reveals that he wanted the musical sequences to function as a Brechtian element in *Head-On*, dividing the text into five structural acts (similar to classical Greek tragedy) and punctuating the beginning of each new act.[9] As such, they also serve as a self-reflexive device directing attention to the staged nature of the text. Musical sequences, I would argue, also insert a certain ambiguity into the film. As a music-inspired film, *Head-On* makes extensive use of an assorted mix of music, presenting its story in such different genres as hard rock, punk, and Turkish popular music.[10] In contrast to this mixture of divergent sounds, the repeated use of what sounds like 'traditional Turkish music' in interludes seems to evoke a sense of authenticity. The repeated use of traditional music, in other words, seems to call attention to an authentic cultural essence in reference to which one must make sense of the story. In reality, however, the music used in the interludes can hardly be considered authentic in the conventional sense of the word. It points not to a unified essence, but to a mixture of dynamic cultural influences. The musicians we see in the interludes are the Roma clarinetist Selim Sesler and his orchestra. Deniz Göktürk (2008) reports that all the interlude songs in the film were chosen from the compilation CD of Selim Sesler and Brenna MacCrimmon, a Canadian researcher and performer who has been researching Roma folk songs in the villages of Turkey and several Balkan countries for the last twenty years.[11] The Roma songs from Brenna MacCrimmon's compilation were re-recorded for the film, performed by Selim Sesler and his orchestra, but with a different vocalist, İdil Üner, a Turkish-German actress who is not a professional singer (Göktürk, 2008). What appears to be 'traditional Turkish music' in the film, then, is an assembly of Roma songs compiled by a Canadian researcher and performed by a Turkish-German actress accompanied by a Roma band. It is also important, according to Göktürk, that the film stages Selim Sesler and his band not as exotic, folkloristic figures, but as distinctly urban musicians in costume and posture; to most spectators, they would at first glance appear indistinguishable from performers of classical Turkish music. 'It is precisely this convergence of intertwined traditions,' Göktürk contends, 'which challenges any nation-based definition of music and, more generally, of culture' (2008: 165). *Head-On*, then, presents a subversive image of Istanbul that turns the clichés about the city upside down. What appears to be an authentic element turns into pure artifice. What appears to be 'traditional culture' is actually all about diversity and fusion. Challenging the notion of an authentic, self-same cultural identity, the film proposes alternative ways of thinking about belonging to a place, culture, and language.[12]

Selim Sesler and his band are one of the many continuous elements between *Head-On* and *Crossing the Bridge*, Akın's following film. Like *Head-On*, *Crossing the Bridge* also challenges the notion of an authentic cultural identity, and turns Istanbul into a dynamic fusion of a multiplicity of sounds and cultural influences. Covering a great variety of music, including hard rock, hip-hop, pop, religious music, arabesque, Kurdish folk music, Roma music, classical Turkish music, and others, the film features many performers, from the legendary stars of Turkish music to unknown street musicians. The diverse music scenes of Istanbul are documented in *Crossing the Bridge* through the narration of a German musician, Alexander Hacke, a member of the experimental band Die Einstürzenden Neubauten. Hacke had previously collaborated with Akın on the soundtrack of *Head-On*.

Several scholars underline the significance of Alexander Hacke's narration/mediation in *Crossing the Bridge*. Fırat Yücel (2005), for example, argues that *Crossing the Bridge* could not have been made by someone who has lived in Istanbul for a long time and closely followed its music scene, since such a person would inevitably have attempted to classify different types of music on the basis of certain pre-established ideas and value judgments prevailing in Turkish culture. Arabesque music, for example, has been regarded for a long time as an inferior cultural form in Turkey by the modernizing cultural elite, who tend to identify themselves with Western classical music. What makes *Crossing the Bridge* refreshing is precisely the absence of these conventional classifications and evaluations. According to Yücel, this is an outcome of Akın's relative distance to Turkey (2005: 45). The narration of Alexander Hacke fosters this quality further in the sense that he looks at the city with a novel perspective not shaped by existing conventions and clichés. Wandering around different parts of the city throughout the film, Hacke seems to feel a genuine enthusiasm for what he is doing. He discovers the urban texture and cultural diversity, meets different musicians, records their music, and takes part in their performances. He shows a heartfelt interest in what different musicians have to say about their city, without any preconceived assumptions in his mind. Similarly, Feride Çiçekoğlu (2007) emphasizes the importance of the 'double outsider/insider position' in the film.[13] As a second-generation member of the Turkish community in Germany, Akın belongs to both cultures, but at the same time he is an outsider to both. He is familiar to Istanbul and Turkish popular culture to an extent, but does not know it all too well. This double viewpoint enables Akın to see Istanbul beyond clichés. He neither tries to reveal the 'truth' of the city, nor is he interested in advancing a grand statement about Istanbul. Instead, he is in search of details, impressions, sounds, and senses. All these minor elements that he emphasizes throughout the film do not necessarily culminate in closure, but create a feeling. There is no truth of the city, the film suggests, beyond a chaotic fusion of influences, interactions, and traditions.

How come, then, that a film so admirably refraining from clichés employs the most tedious of all clichés about Istanbul in its title, namely the metaphor of the bridge? The possible implications of the English title of the film, *Crossing the Bridge*, are quite obvious. Catherine Simpson, for example, reads it as follows:

The English title of the film reflects Turkey's political/cultural/ geographical position at the crossroads at this precise moment. While there is a literal bridge to be 'crossed' by Hacke in *Crossing the Bridge* – the one that straddles the Bosphorus – on the eve of Turkey's accession talks to the European Union, Akın seems to be inviting Western audiences, particularly Europeans, if they can 'cross the bridge.'[14]

Yet, as an explanation of the cultural position of Istanbul (and of Turkey), the metaphor of the bridge is quite problematic in several senses. Meltem Ahıska (2003), for example, talking about the presumed 'in-between' status of Turkey with regard to the East/West divide, asserts:

> Turkey, which has been labeled by both outsiders and insiders as a bridge between the East and the West, has an ambivalent relation not only to the geographical sites of the East and the West, but also to their temporal signification: namely, backwardness and progress. Turkey has been trying to cross the bridge between the East and the West for more than a hundred years now, with a self-conscious anxiety that it is arrested in time and space by the bridge itself. (Ahıska, 2003: 353)

Similarly, Deniz Göktürk (2008) problematizes the English title of the film by suggesting that it is the least convincing aspect of Akın's film. A bridge implies two stable shores. It posits distinct, self-contained continents and cultures: Asia versus Europe, the East versus the West (Göktürk, 2008: 168). While this binary rhetoric is picked up in several conversations with musicians in the film, it is repeatedly deconstructed by foregrounding the mix of musical influences that make up the sound of the city. 'The emphasis in the title,' Göktürk says, 'must therefore be on the "crossing" rather than on the "bridge," on mobility and flux across borders' (2008: 168).

Interestingly, the Turkish title of the film, *Istanbul Hatırası*, is completely different from the English one. It literally means 'memories of Istanbul.' This is also the title of one of the songs performed in the documentary by Sezen Aksu, a legendary female performer and song-writer. The lyrics of her song evoke images of a lost Istanbul, the traces of which can be found only in old black-and-white photos. This melancholic image of Istanbul conjures up the mood that Nobel Prize-winning writer Orhan Pamuk describes in his *Istanbul: Memories and the City* (2005) as *hüzün*, a word that can be translated as a kind of collective melancholy. Pamuk talks about 'the *hüzün* of the entire city of Istanbul' and associates it with the break-up of the Ottoman Empire and modern-day Istanbul's mourning for the loss of its complex multi-cultural identity (2005: 83). In Istanbul, he suggests, the remains of a glorious past and civilization are visible everywhere. These are, however, unlike the remains of great empires seen in Western cities that are preserved in museums and proudly displayed.

> The people of Istanbul simply carry on with their lives amongst the ruins. Many Western writers and travelers find this charming. But for the city's more sensitive and attuned residents, these ruins are reminders that the present city is so poor and confused that it can never again dream of rising to the same heights of wealth, power and culture. (Pamuk, 2005: 91)

Istanbul, according to Pamuk, carries its *hüzün* not as an illness to be cured or a pain to be relieved, but with a sense of pride. It is interesting to note that Pamuk observes in Turkish music a significant manifestation of *hüzün*. 'To varying degrees,' he writes, 'classical Ottoman music, Turkish popular music, especially the arabesk music that became popular during the 1980s, are all expressions of this emotion, which we feel as something in between physical pain and grief' (Pamuk, 2005: 93).

The lyrics of the song 'Memories of Istanbul' certainly evokes a sense of what Orhan Pamuk calls *hüzün*. The song describes a long-forgotten love story. To foster the melancholic aura of the song, old black-and-white images of Istanbul[15] are inserted into Sezen Aksu's live performance. The sense of the past is evoked in the film several times, also through the fragments of old Yeşilçam films inserted into the interviews. For example, in the sequence in which Hacke talks to Orhan Gencebay, the cult figure of arabesque music, we see excerpts from his early films from the 1970s and 1980s. He even shouts at Istanbul in one of these excerpts: 'Istanbul, the aging city, the slut.' These inserts, however, create a sense of irony rather than of a melancholic loss.

Despite the sense of *hüzün* prevailing in several musical performances, I do not think the Turkish title of Akın's film is more apt than the English one in capturing the aura of the documentary. *Crossing the Bridge*, after all, is a film very much preoccupied with the present. Neither the bridge metaphor, nor the melancholy adequately captures the image of Istanbul in Akın's film. I would like to propose a different concept to make sense of the image of the city in *Crossing the Bridge*.

There has long been a battle in Turkey over the metaphors used to describe the cultural make-up of the country. Liberal democrats conventionally describe the multi-cultural history of Turkey through the metaphor of a mosaic. Extreme nationalists, however, challenge this view, claiming that Turkey's cultural character resembles marble rather than a mosaic. The image of marble emphasizes the supposedly undifferentiated, unified character of the nation, and as such it denies the idea of cultural diversity altogether. Compared to marble, the metaphor of the mosaic certainly is more pluralist, yet it is not without its own problems. The different colors of a mosaic are separated from one another with clear boundaries, with no possibility of interaction (Altınay, 2007: 21). In this way, the mosaic metaphor highlights the beauty and richness that emerges from the peaceful co-existence of different cultures. Treating each culture as unique and of equal value to the others, mosaic multi-culturalism connotes cultural homogeneity, boundedness, and distinctness (Altınay, 2007: 21). Recently, the concept of *ebru* – that is, marbled paper, a traditional art form in Turkey – has been proposed as a more fitting metaphor to express Turkey's unique brand of multi-culturalism. This English translation of *ebru* actually conveys very little of the religious, cultural, and historical meanings associated with this symbolically rich Ottoman tradition of artistic expression (Duben, 2007: 65). An *ebru* artist creates his or her drawing with oil-based paint on water and then transfers this floating artwork onto paper. 'Being water-based, an *ebru* connotes fluidity, movement, connectedness, permeability, and contingency' (Altınay, 2007: 19). As a metaphor emphasizing interaction, dialogue, and exchange, it helps us recognize cultural diversity without imprisoning identities into fixed, essentialized entities. What we have in Akın's film, I would argue, is an *ebruesque* Istanbul whose divergent sounds and sensations merge into one another in a continuous motion. The essence of the city, *Crossing the Bridge* suggests, cannot be captured because it is all about fluidity, movement, connectedness, permeability, and contingency.

IV

Apart from the films that put Istanbul at their center, since the mid-2000s another group of films have been made that tell their stories against the backdrop of the city. Giving us a glimpse of certain segments of the city from the perspective of different social groups, these films can also be considered as part of the emerging transnational genre of Istanbul films.[16]

New Istanbul films tackle the clichés about the city. They do not so much negate the clichés as negotiate with them. Acknowledging that it is no longer possible to produce an 'original' image of the city, they recycle the clichés to make new use of them. What is original in new Istanbul films is precisely their reworking of the cliché.[17]

6

THE ABSENT WOMEN OF NEW TURKISH CINEMA

From the perspective of gender relations, new wave Turkish cinema appears to have a rather masculinist outlook. In a great majority of new wave films, 'popular' and 'art' films alike, the story revolves around a male protagonist. Women are portrayed not as active subjects, but as objects of male desire. In fact, it would not be an overstatement to suggest that the absence of women is one of the defining characteristics of new wave cinema.

This absence, I believe, should not necessarily be considered an altogether negative condition in relation to the gender politics of new Turkish cinema. The position of new wave films towards women is shaped around a certain ambivalence. On the one hand, these films subordinate women to men and deny them agency. New Turkish cinema seems disinterested in the stories of women. We never learn how the female character sees the world from her perspective. Without a doubt, this male-dominant attitude is problematic, for it reproduces the still-powerful patriarchal culture in Turkish society. On the other hand, we can also detect a positive element in this masculinist picture, in the sense that new wave films sometimes include a critical self-awareness of their own complicity with patriarchal culture.

I will discuss the ambivalent gender politics of new Turkish cinema through *Vasfiye Is Her Name* (*Adı Vasfiye*), a film made by veteran director Atıf Yılmaz in 1985, a decade before the emergence of the new wave. *Vasfiye Is Her Name* is an important film in Turkish film history, not only because of its innovative cinematic style, but also because of its subversive gender politics. In the following, I will discuss this film as a paradigmatic text that can help to make sense of gender politics in new wave cinema.

I

Apart from being a period of political oppression, the 1980s were also a decade in which new social movements emerged in Turkey. The silencing of leftist politics by the 12 September 1980 coup paradoxically gave rise to new forms of political opposition and social activism. Defining itself as a pluralist, participatory, and de-centered oppositional movement, the feminist movement has brought gender relations onto the political agenda (Tekeli, 1995). Problems such as domestic violence, abortion, and sexual harassment, which had previously been confined to the private domain, began to enter public debate during the 1980s. A variety of women's organizations made efforts to expose gender discrimination in social, political, and legislative domains and struggled to improve the status of women in all areas of life. As an outcome of these efforts, women gained renewed visibility in society. From academic studies to news magazines, from cartoons to literature, gender-related issues have become a popular subject in all realms of cultural life.

This new attention to women had an impact on cinema as well. During the 1980s, 'women's films,' a sub-genre focusing on female characters, appeared in Turkish cinema. Veteran director Atıf Yılmaz is the leading representative of this genre. Among the popular women's films that Atıf Yılmaz directed during this period, one can cite *Mine* (1982), *A Sip of Love* (*Bir Yudum Sevgi*, 1984), *The Untidy Bed* (*Dağınık Yatak*, 1984),

A Widowed Woman (*Dul Bir Kadın*, 1985), *Vasfiye Is Her Name* (*Adı Vasfiye*, 1985), *Oohh Belinda!* (*Aahh Belinda!*, 1986), *How Does Asiye Get Emancipated?* (*Asiye Nasıl Kurtulur?*, 1986), and *Woman Does Not Have a Name* (*Kadının Adı Yok*, 1987). The popularity of Atıf Yılmaz's films encouraged other directors to make films on similar subjects. Ironically, however, the women's films of the 1980s were mostly directed by male directors.

Revolving around female characters, women's films call attention to the different forms of oppression that women experience in Turkish society. The storyline is often shaped around the process of developing a critical self-consciousness about one's life and identity. Becoming aware of their subordinate condition in patriarchal society, female protagonists struggle to take control of their own lives. Women's films introduced realistic female characters to Turkish cinema, very different from the female stereotypes prevailing in Yeşilçam films. The women of the Yeşilçam cinema typically fall into two categories: virtuous or vicious. As opposed to the promiscuous and devious vicious women, virtuous women prove themselves worthy of the love of the male protagonist through their loyalty, devotion, and honor (often equated with virginity). As expected, sexual desire is always a property of vicious women, and extramarital sexuality is seen as sinful. One of the most transgressive aspects of the women's films of the 1980s is their frankness about female sexuality. No longer defined as a matter of chastity, sexuality is presented in these films as an indispensable aspect of women's lives. One can even suggest that women's emancipation in these films is often associated with their sexual awakening. In fact, the most problematic aspect of women's films is also related to their portrayal of female sexuality. While women are represented as active subjects in these films, the female body is often turned into a sexualized spectacle, an object of the voyeuristic male gaze. Despite the centrality of women to the stories, women's films continue to operate within a 'patriarchal regime of looking,' to use Laura Mulvey's well-known expression (1989).

Vasfiye Is Her Name is different from other examples of the genre, in the sense that it brings about a self-conscious critique of the patriarchal gaze inherent in cinema. The story of the film centers not on a female character, but on an absent woman.

Following the credits, *Vasfiye Is Her Name* opens early in the morning, on a large boulevard in Istanbul. Behind cars passing by, there appears a wall partially covered by the posters of a sexy blonde woman, Sevim Suna (Müjde Ar), probably a bar singer. After a while, two men enter the view. We learn from their conversation that the younger one (Erol Durak) is a writer. He complains about not being able to find an interesting subject for his next novel. His friend suggests that everything around them could in fact be a starting point for a novel. To give an example, he points to the posters on the wall. 'Take this woman,' he says, 'who knows what her real name is?' Following this brief conversation, the friend leaves, and the young author gazes at the picture on the wall with growing interest. We see a series of cross-cuts of the man's gaze and the woman's picture. In each cut, we get a closer view of the woman's face. As her eyes fill the screen in the last cut, we hear a muffled male voice in the background. 'Vasfiye,' he says, 'her real name is Vasfiye.' Turning around in bewilderment, the young author comes face to face with a handsome man in his thirties. Introducing himself as Emin (Aytaç Arman), Vasfiye's first husband, the man invites the author to a coffee-house to tell him Vasfiye's real story. We see the events in his narration in a flashback sequence.

Through the day, the protagonist meets four different men, each claiming to know Vasfiye's real story, and each telling a different version of her life story, rendered in a flashback sequence. Although each story covers a different time period, they sometimes overlap. Some parts of the stories complement, others contradict each other. From Emin's story, we learn that Vasfiye and Emin used to be childhood sweethearts. They married in their early twenties and moved to a larger town to get away from Emin's abusive family. Listening to Emin's story with great interest, the protagonist turns around for a moment to order another glass of tea. When he turns back, Emin has disappeared. After a short while, a skinny middle-aged man shows up, introducing himself as Rüstem (Macit Koper). He narrates a different version of the woman's life. In Rüstem's story, we learn that he was a healthcare worker in a dispensary in the town to which Emin and Vasfiye moved. He describes Emin as an adulterous and violent husband who beat his wife. Vasfiye meets Rüstem at the dispensary, where she goes for treatment for the bruises on her body. She invites him to her home and seduces him. Confused by this story, the protagonist goes outside for some fresh air. By then, it is already evening. As he walks along the narrow backstreets of Beyoğlu, an elderly man knocks on the window of a small restaurant and invites him in. This is Hamza (Levent Yılmaz), Vasfiye's second husband. Hamza's narration discredits the events in Rüstem's story. Now we are told that Rüstem's feelings for Vasfiye were not reciprocated. He fantasizes about having an affair with her and tells everyone about an imagined affair as if it was real. Hearing the rumors about his wife cheating on him, Emin stabs both Rüstem and Vasfiye out of jealousy. Hamza meets Vasfiye at the hospital where she is being treated. Upon her recovery, she divorces Emin, who already is in jail. Hamza helps Vasfiye to find a job at a hairdresser, and after a while they marry. Hamza wants his young and attractive wife to lead a strictly conservative lifestyle and to stay at home. Meanwhile, Emin is released from prison and becomes a minibus driver in the same town. After their first encounter, Vasfiye and Emin rekindle their love and escape together. At this point of his story, Hamza excuses himself to visit the lavatory and never returns.

All the more confused, the protagonist decides to go to the nightclub where Vasfiye/Sevim Suna performs. There, a melancholic young man approaches him, saying that he has been waiting for him. This is Fuat (Yılmaz Zafer), a young doctor and Vasfiye's lover in the town where she worked in a hairdressing salon after Emin was imprisoned for some petty crime. In his story, Fuat tells how much he was in love with Vasfiye, how happy they were until Emin found Vasfiye again. Towards the end of Fuat's story, Sevim Suna's name is announced, and she appears on stage. Fuat wants the protagonist to pass a folded note to Vasfiye; 'Only you can help me,' he says. Under the influence of Fuat's touching story, the protagonist approaches Vasfiye/Sevim Suna in a mesmerized state and hands over the note. When she opens the paper, however, it turns out that nothing is written on it. The protagonist turns around and notices that Fuat is no longer at the table. In panic, he hastily tries to explain himself to the woman. He says he knows everything about her, he knows that she is Vasfiye, that she is in love with Fuat. Sevim Suna/Vasfiye does not seem to care much about what he is saying. As the protagonist insistently pursues her, the waiter intervenes and holds him back, saying that they have had enough of him creating the same disturbance every night. In the next scene, the protagonist finds Sevim Suna backstage. He begs her to talk to him; 'This is your life,' he says, 'you are the one who should talk.' The woman again does not pay much attention to him. Meanwhile, Emin steps into the room and, ignoring the protagonist, talks directly to Sevim Suna/Vasfiye. He says a man is waiting for her at the hotel. Realizing that Emin is selling her to men, the protagonist loses his temper and hits Emin, with the words 'I won't allow you to make her a prostitute.' After a moment of hesitation, Emin stabs him in the stomach. Both Emin and Sevim Suna/Vasfiye act as if this is a casual incident. Before leaving the room, Sevim Suna/Vasfiye hands a red rose to the protagonist, with a sympathetic yet jaded smile on her face.

In the final scene, we see the protagonist the next morning, on the same spot where he first saw Sevim Suna's posters. Leaning against the wall slightly bent over, he is in the same position as he was after having been stabbed. His older friend anxiously approaches him and asks whether he is all right. As the protagonist straightens up, we realize that there is no wound on his body. 'Did you find her?' his friend asks. 'Vasfiye is her name,' replies the protagonist. 'I could not find her, but I certainly will,' he adds. As he begins to walk the street alone, he takes a red rose out of his jacket and smells it. The frame showing him as he smells the rose freezes and shatters like a mirror.

In *Vasfiye Is Her Name*, dramatic tension arises from the act of solving a puzzle, revealing the truth behind a mystery. The riddle around which the narrative is organized is introduced in the opening sequence as the true identity of the woman on the poster. The male protagonist is positioned as the narrative subject with whose gaze we can identify in the process of solving the puzzle. Setting aside the opening and the final sequences, the main body of the narrative is composed of four stories told by four different men involved in the woman's life at different periods of time. These are mainly sequential stories that seem to provide a plausible picture of the woman's life. When considering these four stories together, in other words, one can get a general idea about the identity of the woman on the poster, about the events she has been through, and how she ended up in her present situation. This is not a coherent picture, however. Although the course of events seems to be logical, we get the sense that each story is about a different woman. In Emin's story, we see a candid and funny young girl, whereas in Rüstem's she turns into a seductive temptress. Hamza's story is about a vulnerable, helpless victim, while in Fuat's narration we encounter a mature woman who frankly expresses her desire and sexuality. In each story, the woman takes on a different identity on the basis of the perspective of the male narrator. The narrative is destabilized by the fact that the enigma ultimately remains unsolved; the truth of the woman is never revealed, her identity cannot be fixed. Thus, the film frustrates the desire that it has stimulated in the first place.

Apart from the riddle that remains unsolved, what further destabilizes the narrative in *Vasfiye Is Her Name* is the subject who attempts to solve it. In the opening sequence, the young author appears to be a reliable narrative subject with whom to identify. He will investigate, we assume, the identity of the woman from an objective standpoint. At that stage, the object and the subject of investigation seem to be clearly separated from one another. As the narrative progresses, however, the protagonist loses his detached position and gradually becomes a part of the enigma he is supposed to solve. While he listens to Emin's story as an outsider at the beginning, he seems to be already involved in the woman's life when talking to Fuat at the end. The way in which he is treated by the waiter in the nightclub, as someone stalking Sevim Suna, raises the question as to whether it is the protagonist himself who has imagined everything in the first place. All this suggests that there is an unstable subject at the center of the narrative. Rendering the position of the narrative subject suspicious, the film blurs the line between reality and fantasy. It casts doubt on the validity of the stories not only of the four men involved in the woman's life, but also of that of the protagonist.

The *mise-en-scène* also contributes to the blurring line between reality and fantasy. The mirror is a recurring motif in *Vasfiye Is Her Name*. In all the scenes showing the protagonist conversing with the men involved in the woman's life – the coffee-house, the restaurant, and the nightclub – mirrors are present. In these scenes, we sometimes only see the mirror reflection of the image, at other times the image is duplicated or multiplied by its reflection. Likewise, the entire scene depicting the events taking place in Sevim Suna's dressing room is shown as reflected in a large mirror on the wall. As indicated above, the last image of the film is a freeze-frame shattering like a mirror. The use of mirrors in all of these scenes divides, multiplies, alters, and distorts the image. In most scenes, we cannot tell which image is real and which is a reflection. The excessive use of mirrors in the *mise-en-scène* contributes to the blurring of the line between reality and illusion and destabilizes the narrative.

The ultimate shattering of reality in *Vasfiye Is Her Name*, however, comes with the final sequence in which the two material signs that could prove or falsify the validity of the protagonist's story testify in opposite directions: the stab wound on the body of the protagonist mysteriously disappears, while the rose remains with him. It is no longer possible to know what is real and what is imaginary.

How, then, can we make sense of the self-reflexive aspects of *Vasfiye Is Her Name*? What is the connection between the story of the film and its self-conscious mode of storytelling? I think the peculiar use of self-reflexivity in *Vasfiye Is Her Name* can be more clearly understood when considered in relation to its gender politics.

II

In *Invisible Cities*, Italo Calvino describes the foundation of the city of Zobeide as follows:

> [. . .] men of various nations had an identical dream. They saw a woman running at night through an unknown city; she was seen from behind, with long hair, and she was naked. They dreamed of pursuing her. As they twisted and turned, each of them lost her. After the dream they set out in search of that city; they never found it, but they found one another; they decided to build a city like the one in the dream. In laying out the streets, each followed the course of his pursuit; at the spot where they had lost the fugitive's trail, they arranged spaces and walls differently from the dream, so she would be unable to escape again.
>
> This was the city of Zobeide, where they settled, waiting for that scene to be repeated one night. None of them, asleep or awake, ever saw the woman again. The city's streets were streets where they went to work every day, with no link anymore to the dreamed chase. Which, for that matter, had long been forgotten.
>
> New men arrived from other lands, having had a dream like theirs, and in the city of Zobeide, they recognized something of the streets of the dream, and they changed the positions of arcades and stairways to resemble more closely the path of the pursued woman and so, at the spot where she had vanished, there would remain no avenue of escape.

The first to arrive could not understand what drew these people to
Zobeide, this ugly city, this trap. (Calvino, 1974: 45–6)

Discussing Calvino's text, Teresa de Lauretis asserts that the
tale of Zobeide tells the story of the production of woman as
text (1984: 13). The city of Zobeide is in fact a representation of
woman, and woman is the ground of that representation. Being
both the foundation and the very condition of representation,
the woman, for whom the city is built, however, is nowhere in
the city. 'In endless circularity [. . .] the woman is at once the
dream's object of desire and the reason for its objectification:
the construction of the city. She is both the source of the drive
to represent and its ultimate, unattainable goal. Thus the city,
which is built to capture men's dream, finally only inscribes
woman's absence' (De Lauretis, 1984: 12–13). Elsewhere, De
Lauretis talks about a similar paradox in relation to the concept
of the 'non-being of woman,' which refers to 'the paradox of a
being that is at once captive and absent in discourse, constantly
spoken of but of itself inaudible or inexpressible, displayed as
spectacle and still unrepresented or unrepresentable, invisible
yet constituted as the object and the guarantee of vision; a being
whose existence and specificity are simultaneously asserted, and
denied, negated and controlled' (De Lauretis, 1990: 115).

The narrative structure of *Vasfiye Is Her Name* resembles
the story of the foundation of the city in Calvino's tale. The
narrative progresses in the film, just as in the tale, in pursuit of
a woman. In the opening sequence, the image of the woman is
presented as an inspiration for the process of artistic production.
The young author who looks for an interesting subject for his
next novel begins to pursue this image. The dream of capturing
the woman (solving her mystery, revealing her true identity) is
both the starting point and the ultimate goal of the narrative.
Then, however, the protagonist himself begins to be gradually
possessed by his own desire. The pursuit of the woman leads
him not to the woman, but to other men. Eventually, he gets

lost in this impossible endeavor. Just like in Calvino's tale, the woman in *Vasfiye Is Her Name* is present, not as a being, but as an image, a story, a dream. In the discourses of men, the woman constantly takes on new identities. Yet, in a world replete with her image, the woman is an absentee. She is constantly spoken of, but does not have a voice to tell her own story. We never know what she thinks, feels, or wishes.

Vasfiye Is Her Name is a text that is self-conscious not only about its own constructed nature, but also about its complicity with the patriarchal system of representation. The film is not about a woman, but about the process of representing the woman. There is an absent woman at the center of the story. The film makes use of several self-reflexive strategies to make visible this constitutive absence at its core. The subversive side of the film becomes manifest most clearly in the protagonist's words in Sevim Suna's dressing room. After begging her to talk to him, he continues: 'Everyone has said something about you, but this is your life, you are the one who should talk . . .' The protagonist notices the irony of the situation: the woman's story is told by men. Her identity is defined, controlled, and fixed by men. Yet the irony is not limited to this. After all, is the protagonist's position any different from that of the other men involved in the woman's life? Is he not also telling his own story to fill the woman's silence? Is it not true that the desire to represent the woman is an extension of the desire to confine and control her? And finally, is this not also the case for the representation of women in the genre of women's films of the 1980s?

III

When we look at the representations of women in new Turkish cinema, it is possible to detect an attitude similar to the one in *Vasfiye Is Her Name*. The figure of woman in new wave films, as in *Vasfiye Is Her Name*, often comes into view as a constitutive absence. She is the driving force behind the narrative, yet absent as a subject. She is constantly spoken of by men, yet her own voice cannot possibly be heard. Visible as a sexualized spectacle, she is not granted any agency. In new wave films, the figure of woman becomes a ground on which men confront, challenge, and dispute one another. In a world populated by her own image, the woman is present as a 'non-being.' She is inscribed as an absence in the story for which she has been the driving force. New Turkish cinema speaks over the silence of women. Again and again, we encounter mute women in these films.

A case in point is Serdar Akar's 1998 film, *On Board* (*Gemide*). The film opens with the line 'A boat is like a country.' Focusing on conflicting relations among a group of seamen on a cargo ship, *On Board* uses the enclosed world of the boat as a microcosm representing larger society. The ground on which men confront and challenge each another in this microcosm is the body of a woman, a Romanian prostitute, who has been abducted and taken hostage on board. As she is repeatedly raped, she never speaks, not only because she is gagged most of the time, but also because she does not know the language. Over the last decades, Istanbul has been host to many women brought from former Eastern Bloc countries for prostitution. In this way, the city has ironically realized its aspiration to become a global center – first in the business of trafficking women. The Romanian prostitute at the center of the flim's narrative is one of these women. As her body becomes a battleground for the men to act out the power struggle among themselves, we never get to learn what she feels or thinks. The men constantly speak of her and try to solve her mystery. They speculate about her real identity. Is she a virgin or a whore, an innocent victim or a filthy slut? She takes different identities in the narrations of the men. Employing a masculine language full of misogynist idioms, *On Board* quite self-consciously reduces the woman at the center of its story into a sexualized object. The film neither attempts to give her a voice nor a subject position. It is not easy to assess, however, to what extent we can take this self-conscious attitude as a subversive

174

element in relation to the film's gender politics. Turning the violation of the female body into a sexualized spectacle and taking a voyeuristic position, the film seems to reproduce rather than criticize the patriarchal ideology that it so vividly portrays.

It would be unfair to suggest that the dark masculinist discourse dominating *On Board* is shared by all new wave films. Nevertheless, it is true that women are absent in a majority of these films. From the young woman in Derviş Zaim's *Somersault in the Coffin*, to the femme fatale character in Zeki Demirkubuz' *The Third Page*, from the mysterious lover in Nuri Bilge Ceylan's *Distant* to the disabled daughter of the librarian in Yılmaz Erdoğan's *Vizontele Tuuba* – female characters, in popular and art films alike, are always represented as they are seen by men. Films seem to withdraw self-consciously from the domain of women and focus on the stories of men. In some of these films, we can discern a subtle critique of the films' complicity with the patriarchal culture prevailing in Turkey. Yet, in the final analysis, these films are about men, and women leak into the stories only as objects of male desire.

What about films made by female directors? For one, the number of women directors in Turkish cinema is quite limited.[1] The few women who are currently active in cinema – such as Yeşim Ustaoğlu, Handan İpekçi, Tomris Giritlioğlu, and Biket İlhan – often downplay the question of gender in their films. Even in films such as *Waiting for the Clouds*, where stories revolve around female characters, the filmmakers seem to shy away from foregrounding gender-related issues.[2] Consistent with this observation, women directors often tend to distance themselves from a feminist position. In fact, usually they do not even like to be called 'women directors.' Making powerful political films such as *Journey to the Sun* and *Waiting for the Clouds*, Yeşim Ustaoğlu, for example, expresses a decided distaste for being confined to the category of 'woman director' and indicates that she considers herself solely a 'filmmaker.' When asked in an interview whether she has experienced advantages or disadvantages as a woman director, she replied that gender does not matter; 'an artist is an artist' (quoted by Öztürk, 2004: 343).

As I have argued elsewhere, Ustaoğlu's reactionary response can be understood in the context of the restraining expectations placed especially on third-world female artists (Suner, 2007). Writing on the reception of third-world women writers in the West, Amal Amireh and Lisa Suhair Majaj (2000) have argued that, instead of being received as artworks, third-world women's texts are viewed primarily as sociological treatises granting Western readers a glimpse into the 'oppression' of third-world women. Muslim women of the Middle East especially, according to Amireh and Majaj, are typically seen as victims of religion, patriarchy, tradition, and poverty in the West, and women artists from this region are expected to testify to this presumed condition. Although they do not see themselves merely as Middle Eastern, Muslim, third-world women, these artists are viewed as only that and denied an identity in the plural (Amireh and Majaj, 2000: 1–2). In the light of this discussion, we can understand why Yeşim Ustaoğlu, like several other contemporary women directors of Turkish cinema, dislikes being characterized as a 'woman director.'

Having drawn a rather pessimistic picture so far, I would like to conclude this chapter by calling attention to a promising development in relation to the gender politics of new Turkish cinema. In recent years, a younger generation of women directors has emerged: a generation of women that seem to be more comfortable with foregrounding gender-related issues in their films and identifying themselves with a feminist position. Making short and/or documentary films, these directors usually offer subversive strategies of disrupting patriarchal culture in Turkey. I would like to mention Pelin Esmer and Eylem Kaftan among the most interesting names of this new generation of women directors. In stark contrast to the dominant tendency in new wave Turkish cinema, Pelin Esmer and Eylem Kaftan are preoccupied with problematizing the silencing of women in Turkish society. Pelin Esmer's 2005 feature-length documentary *Play* (*Oyun*) is about a group of women in a small mountain village in southern Turkey, who attempt to stage a play about their own lives. As the women discuss their forced marriages, abusive husbands, manipulative in-laws, and so forth, Esmer with her camera bears witness to the process of the rehearsals and the staging of a drama entitled 'The Outcry of Women.' In this drama, women play all the roles, both male and female. The process of staging a play also turns out to be a process of transformation for the women. They build a new self-confidence and strength out of this communal endeavor. Talking about how her film blurs the lines between the lives of the women and their play, fiction and reality, film and play, Esmer says: 'I wanted to shoot a fiction-like documentary rather than a documentary-like fiction film, without trying to be invisible, but quietly integrating myself in [the women's] lives [. . .].'[3] On the whole, Esmer's film is a celebration of the empowerment of women, which comes with finding their own voice and making themselves heard.

Eylem Kaftan's 2005 documentary *Vendetta Song* (*İsmi Güzide*) describes the filmmaker's journey from Montreal all the way to a remote Kurdish village close to Diyarbakır in order to solve the thirty-year-old mystery of the murder of her aunt Güzide, the victim of an honor killing. During her journey, Kaftan finds out not only about her aunt's long-forgotten life, but also about the realities of women's lives in rural Turkey, which do not seem to have changed much in the past three decades. Arranged marriages, blood feuds, and honor killings are still a part of women's lives, and young girls are forced to drop out of school at an early age to look after their siblings and are given away as brides in exchange for a payment to their families. Kaftan's film, in this sense, is not just about the silencing of women in the past, but also in the present. 'I feel I owe something to these women,' she says, 'my work is a way of empowering myself and hoping it will touch other lives.'[4] Interestingly enough, there is an absent woman at the center of Kaftan's film – Güzide, the murdered aunt – and the narrative is organized around the impulse of solving the mystery behind her life and death. There is also an interesting parallel between the film's Turkish title (which literally means 'Güzide Is Her Name') and the title of Atıf Yılmaz's film, *Vasfiye Is Her Name*. However, unlike *Vasfiye Is Her Name* and the new wave films that share a similar structure, Kaftan's film has a woman (the director herself) as the narrative subject, and she powerfully problematizes a patriarchal culture in Turkey that renders her aunt, like many other women, absent.[5]

It is to be hoped that the masculinist discourse of new Turkish cinema will change in the years to come, with the possible entrance of young women directors like Pelin Esmer and Eylem Kaftan onto the feature filmmaking scene.

AFTERWORD

In *Minima Moralia*, Theodor Adorno writes about Nietzsche's contention that not owning a house is even part of his good fortune.[1] 'Today, we should have to add,' he claims, 'it is part of morality not to be at home in one's home' (Adorno, 2002[first published 1951]: 39). Adorno makes this assertion after looking at the new modern world that has been reconstructed after World War II, the concentration camps, and the destruction of European cities by heavy bombardment. At a time when traditional houses have grown intolerable, because 'each trait of comfort in them is paid for with a betrayal of knowledge, each vestige of shelter with the musty pact of family interests,' and when modern functional residences have been designed as 'living cases manufactured by experts for philistines, or factory sites that have strayed into the consumption sphere, devoid of all relation to the occupant,' Adorno declares the impossibility of dwelling in the proper sense (Adorno, 2002: 38). 'The house,' he writes, 'is past' (Adorno, 2002: 39). Etienne Balibar, who looked at the modern world in the age of globalization, writes almost half a century after Adorno: 'Hence the ever recurring paradox of nationalism: the regressive imagining of a nation-state where the individuals would by their nature be "at home," because they would be "among their own" (their own kind), and the rendering of that state uninhabitable [. . .]' (Balibar, 1992: 215).

New wave Turkish films remind me of these observations made in different historical circumstances on the impossibility of home in our contemporary world. Many of the new wave films of the last decade bring us back 'home' and force us to reconsider our relationship of belonging. We encounter home in different manifestations in these films. Sometimes it manifests itself as a dream that leads us towards reconciliation with the past; a dream that softens the disturbing specter of the past, that repairs our damaged sense of self, that envelops us with a sense of innocence. At other times, home turns into a defeatist, irreconcilable place that pulls us into the cul-de-sac of belonging; it simultaneously becomes our shelter and our prison. Sometimes, there is more to it: home is hell, torture; wherever we go, we encounter a curse that does not let us go. Home always co-exists with its exterior, with those who were left outside, those who were not accepted inside. Sometimes, when our home is the homelessness of others, we only see a blind hole, a void. From whichever angle we look at home, it never is only home itself. There are always cracks in it, and from these cracks leak the traces of other pasts, other memories, other experiences. Adopting Zizek's assertion, we can suggest that 'there is no home without the spectre' (2000: 21).[2]

Writing on the recent state of Turkish society, Ayşe Gül Altınay (2007) suggests: 'Turkey is experiencing the painful, yet very creative process of transformation from a plural to a pluralist polity and society. There are many dilemmas and a heavy historical burden to address in this process' (2007: 23). New wave Turkish cinema, I would like to add, contributes to this process by offering new ways of thinking about the 'impossibility of home' in contemporary Turkey. Discovering the impossibility of home after all may not necessarily be a negative last point, a moment of closure. Sometimes this discovery is rather the beginning of a journey, a journey opening up new possibilities, ideas, and dreams.

NOTES

INTRODUCTION

1 Dilek Kaya Mutlu (2007) reveals that, apart from the ambiguity of its existence, the content of *The Demolition of the Russian Monument at San Stefano* is also quite curious. In 1898, a Russian monument was erected at Ayastefanos (San Stefano, present-day Yeşilköy, a district on the southwestern outskirts of Istanbul) to commemorate the Russian victory in the 1877–78 Russo-Ottoman War. In November of 1914, soon after the Ottoman Empire's entry into World War I as Germany's ally, the government staged a propaganda event to motivate the public, and the Russian monument was dynamited by Turkish troops. The Ottoman press welcomed this event at the time, since the monument was the symbol of a bad memory of defeat. The monument was almost forgotten until the mid-1940s, when the first survey of the history of Turkish cinema was published. This survey mentions an early event during which a Turkish army officer filmed the demolition of the Russian monument. Throughout the 1950s and 1960s, this brief note on Fuat Uzkınay was transformed in the hands of Turkish film historians into a nationalist heroic narrative of the beginning of Turkish cinema (Kaya Mutlu, 2007: 75). What makes this story surely ironic is the strange course of events: first the erection of a monument for the remembrance of a victory, then its destruction in order to erase the memory of a defeat; the filming of the monument's destruction for the remembrance of this very event; the disappearance (or non-existence) of the film that is assumed to have recorded the act of destruction; and finally the elevation of an absent film to the status of the monumental beginning of Turkish film history.

2 A recent discovery suggests that it was the brothers Milton and Yanaki Manaki (Ottoman citizens of Greek origin) who made the first Ottoman film in 1911 (Erdoğan and Göktürk, 2001: 533–4). This film consists of documentary footage showing Sultan Mehmed V (Reshad)'s visit to Manastir and Salonika. This film is available in the Macedonia Film Archive. Historians probably did not consider this film as the appropriate beginning of Turkish cinema because the filmmakers were non-Muslim Ottoman citizens of Greek origin (Kaya Mutlu, 2007: 82).

3 Sigmund Weinberg completed *The Marriage of Himmet Agha* (*Himmet Ağanın İzdivacı*) in 1916. This was followed by two films by Sedat Simavi, a young journalist: *The Claw* (*Pençe*, 1917) and *The Spy* (*Casus*, 1917). The veteran stage actor and director Ahmet Fehim made three films in the following years: *The Governess* (*Mürebbiye*, 1919), *Binnaz* (1919) and *Custodian Bican* (*Bican Efendi Vekilharç*, 1921).

4 Yılmaz Güney was arrested in 1974 for killing a judge during a late-night drunken fight in a restaurant while he was shooting *Anxiety*. Bilge Ebiri suggests that, although the details of this event are still unclear, much of Güney's mythology today rests on the belief that Güney was wrongfully convicted (Bilge Ebiri, 'Yılmaz Güney,' *Senses of Cinema*, September 2005, http://www.sensesofcinema.com/contents/directors/05/guney.html. Accessed 6 January 2008).

5 Yılmaz Güney shared the Palme d'Or at the 1982 Cannes Film Festival with Costa Gavras' *Missing*.

6 The issue of Güney's authorship of the films he did not technically direct is a controversial one. At the 1982 Cannes Film Festival, it was producer Yılmaz Güney, not director Şerif Gören, who received the Palme d'Or for *The Way*. Still, Güney is thought to have had a unique amount of control over his remote sets. Bilge Ebiri reports that Güney was allowed to watch dailies, order reshooting, and even edit in prison (Bilge Ebiri, 'Yılmaz Güney,' *Senses of Cinema*, September 2005, http://www.sensesofcinema.com/contents/directors/05/guney. html. Accessed 6 January 2008.)

7 I have argued elsewhere that, despite the powerful presence of Yılmaz Güney in Turkish film history, his cinema has not received the kind of critical attention it deserves. For the Turkish right wing, Güney was a dissident who betrayed his country abroad. For the left wing, he was a political *auteur* who bravely stood up for the oppressed classes. Recently, Kurdish nationalists appropriated Güney as a Kurdish director who until the end of his life was never

allowed to express his true identity. What was largely lost in this debate, however, were Güney's films themselves, which rarely received critical attention beyond unconditional applause or total condemnation (Suner, 1998).

8 The conflict between Kurdish seperatist guerillas (Kurdistan Workers' Party, PKK) and the Turkish army dates back to the 1980s. The PKK initiated an armed struggle against the state in 1984, and Turkish security forces intensified their struggle against the PKK within the framework of the state of emergency declared in 1987. The inhabitants of many rural settlements were evicted during the state of emergency.

9 The terms 'new wave cinema' and 'new cinema' are often used interchangeably to refer to cinematic movements initiated by a new generation of directors who represent a novel approach to filmmaking. The term 'new wave' is conventionally associated with the French new wave (*nouvelle vague*), the film movement of 1960s France. The term refers to films made by a new generation of French filmmakers who went against the prevailing trends in the French cinema of the 1950s, a cinema that had been labeled by the *Cahiers du Cinéma* critics as the '*cinéma de papa*' (daddy's cinema) (Hayward, 1996: 136). The French new wave itself was largely inspired by the Italian neo-realist movement of the 1940s and the early 1950s, characterized by a commitment to the realistic representation of the social world. The Italian neo-realism and the French new wave fueled a new kind of cinema across the globe that often entailed a critical social standpoint and cinematic experimentation. In Brazil, for example, this tendency was carried out by a realist and political new wave movement throughout the 1950s and the 1960s known as *Cinema Novo*. By the early 1970s, a powerful cinematic movement came into being in Germany known as 'new German cinema' whose roots go back to the early 1960s when twenty-six young filmmakers signed the Oberhausen Manifesto in 1962, swearing a death to the established film industry in Germany (which was called *Papas Kino*, daddy's cinema) and announcing the birth of a new and a more political cinema (Hayward, 1996: 168). Starting from the 1980s, new wave movements began to appear among non-Western cinemas, most notably in Iran, Hong Kong, and Taiwan. Unlike the previous new wave movements, these 'new cinemas' are characterized not so much by a clearly defined political standpoint, but rather by a more ambivalent position with regard to social issues.

183

10 Box-office rates are acquired from: '*Kurtlar Vadisi Irak* Tüm Rekorları Kırdı,' *Milliyet*, 8 March 2006, http://www.milliyet.com.tr/2006/03/08/magazin/amag.html. Accessed 7 March 2009.

11 Among the directors of the new popular cinema mentioned in this chapter, Mustafa Altıoklar, Sinan Çetin, and Yavuz Turgul are exceptions in the sense that, unlike other new wave directors, they made their first feature films before the mid-1990s.

12 http://www.medyaline.com/yazdir.asp?hid=1856. Accessed 20 February 2008.

13 Ibid.

14 Ibid.

15 Ibid.

16 *Milliyet*, 8 March 2006, http://www.milliyet.com/2006/03/08/magazin/amag.html. Accessed 7 January 2007.

17 Mehmet Emin Toprak tragically died in a car crash after *Distant* was selected for the 2003 Cannes Festival.

18 On 25 May 2008, Nuri Bilge Ceylan won the Best Director Award at the 2008 Cannes Film Festival for *Three Monkeys* (*Üç Maymun*). This film was released after the time of this writing.

19 Atıf Yılmaz died in May 2006, at the age of 81.

CHAPTER 1

1 Another film that can be included in this list is *Summer Love* (*O da Beni Seviyor*, Barış Pirhasan, 2001). Revolving around a teenage love affair in a village in Malatya during the 1970s, *Summer Love* recounts a rather personal story when compared to the community-based stories of other nostalgia films. For more discussion on *Summer Love* see Suner (2002).

2 During the last decade, a group of films that can be classified as historical films were also made in Turkey. Ziya Öztan's *The Republic* (*Cumhuriyet*, 1998) and *The Fall of Abdülhamit* (*Abdülhamit Düşerken*, 2003) are films that seek to give an objective historical account of the final years of the Ottoman Empire, the War of Independence and the subsequent constitution of the Republic. Mostly reproducing the official historical account, these films, and particularly *The Republic*, are still shown on television and in schools on days of national commemoration. A more recent example of a historical film is *Zincirbozan* (Atıl İnaç, 2007), which narrates the background events to the 12 September 1980 military intervention. The film

suggests that the social turmoil and political assassinations that led to the coup were part of an American conspiracy.

3 The term 'nostalgia cinema' is usually associated with Fredric Jameson's well-known discussion of postmodernism. According to Jameson (1983, 1991), one distinguishing characteristic of our contemporary postmodern age is the weakening of 'historicity.' Nostalgia cinema reconstructs the past through a series of images without historical depth. In these films, history turns out to be an illusive phantasm of the styles of the past that can be reproduced for consumption in the cultural commodity market. Drawing upon a group of American films of the 1980s, Jameson produces an apparently negative account of nostalgia cinema which he perceives as a potent symptom of postmodern culture's inability to cope with time and history. Jameson's critical take on nostalgia cinema is challenged by several scholars. Linda Hutcheon (1988, 1989), for example, criticizes Jameson for disregarding the subversive potential of the textual strategies that postmodern texts employ. According to Hutcheon, postmodern art's deliberate refusal to offer historicity arises from the recognition that the social, historical, and existential 'reality' of the past is a discursive reality when it is used as a referent of art. The only 'genuine historicity' is that which would openly acknowledge its own discursive, contingent identity (Hutcheon, 1988: 24). Applying the notion of nostalgia film to the study of the post-1984 Hong Kong cinema, Natalia Chan Sui Hung (2000) tends to agree with Hutcheon's argument. She indicates that nostalgia cinema, far from effacing historicity, may indeed provide an opportunity to rewrite history and collective memory.

4 Unlike most other nostalgia films, *Propaganda* has a happy ending. In the conclusion, the customs officer, despite the protests of his deputy, joins the townspeople and demolishes the barbed wire with them.

5 Osman Sınav, interviewed by Ebru Çapa, *Aktüel* 602 (2003). The quotation is taken from Zeynep Gültekin, 'Irak'dan Önce: Kurtlar Vadisi Dizisi,' *İletişim Kuram ve Araştırma Dergisi* 22 (2006): 9–36, http://www.ilet.gazi.edu.tr/iletisim_dergi/22/2.pdf. Accessed 29 November 2007.

CHAPTER 2

1 Starting in the mid-1990s, the number of missing persons has gradually dropped, and the problem seems to have been solved

to a great extent by the 2000s. 'Türkiye'de Gözaltında Kayıplar,' *Bianet*, 25 January 2005, http://www.bianet.org/bianet/yazdir/52998. Accessed 26 December 2007.

2 *Mehmet's Book* has so far been translated into five languages and published in several European countires. It was published in English under the title *Voices from the Front: Turkish Soldiers on the War with the Kurdish Guerillas* (Palgrave MacMillan, 2005).

3 New political films can also be studied in relation to the concept of 'trauma cinema,' which refers to films dealing with traumatic events, often in a nonrealistic mode. 'Trauma films,' according to Janet Walker, tend to 'disremember' the past by drawing on innovative strategies for representing reality obliquely, by looking to mental processes for inspiration, and by incorporating self-reflexive devices (Walker, 2005: 19). Among the films discussed here, *Toss Up* especially is consistent with this description.

4 *Mud* is in fact one part of a trilogy produced in collaboration by two Cypriot filmmakers, Derviş Zaim and Panikos Chrissanthou, whose life stories have parallel experiences of displacement. Zaim's family fled their homes in the south in 1974, while Chrissanthou was forced to abandon his in the north. The second part of the trilogy, *Parallel Trips* (*Paralel Yolculuklar*, 2004) co-directed by Zaim and Chrissanthou, is a documentary made up of a series of anecdotes narrated by Turkish and Greek Cypriots who experienced the violent clashes of 1974. The third part, *Akamas* (2006), is a feature film directed by Chrissanthou, about a love story between a Turkish Cypriot boy and a Greek Cypriot girl.

5 Ayşe Gül Altınay, 'Türkiyeli Ermenilerin Yeniden Keşfi' (unpublished paper). İmparatorluğun Çöküş Döneminde Osmanlı Ermenileri: Bilimsel Sorumluluk ve Demokrasi Sorunları Konferansı. Istanbul Bilgi University, Istanbul, 24–5 September 2005.

6 Challenging the notions of national belonging and identity, new political films are often unpopular with the authorities. They may not face direct censorship, but they often encounter sanctions because of their subversive political content. Derviş Zaim, for example, shot only a small part of *Mud* in northern Cyprus, for fear of alerting the authorities to its content. Most parts of the film were shot in different locations in Turkey. Similarly, although *Journey to the Sun* did not confront direct censorship, Yeşim Ustaoğlu had difficulties in distributing her film in Turkey. The local distributors in Turkey, both Turkish and American, remained reluctant to release it in the

tense atmosphere marked by the bomb attacks after the arrest of the PKK leader Abdullah Öcalan in February 1999. After more than a year of negotiations, the film was finally released in a limited circuit of independent movie theaters with eight prints, in March of 2000 (Monceau, 2001: 28). When asked whether she had difficulties with censorship, Ustaoğlu replied: 'At one point the shooting was stopped, and we could only start again three months later. When we finished the movie, we applied for the release permission from the Ministry of Cultural Affairs and we got it without difficulties. This was after the World Premiere at the 1999 Berlin Film Festival, where the movie was awarded two prices (Best European Film and the Peace Prize). Then the 1999 Ankara and Istanbul Film Festivals showed the film. We had begun discussions with the distributors but all the doors were closed. We faced an "embargo" against the film from the major distributors. After a year, we didn't want to wait anymore, because the subject was so timely, so we decided to distribute the film ourselves. We contacted small cinemas in Istanbul, Ankara, Diyarbakır, and other cities where we opened the movie. In four months, more than 70,000 people in Turkey have seen the film' (reported by Monceau, 2001: 29).

CHAPTER 3

1 Ceylan's 2008 film *Three Monkeys* (*Üç Maymun*), which won the Best Director Award at the 2008 Cannes Film Festival, was released after the time of this writing.
2 Jonas Milk, 'On Relationships: An Interview With Nuri Bilge Ceylan,' *Little White Lies* 10 (February–March 2007). http://www.nbcfilm.com/iklimler/press_littlewhitelies.php. Accessed 26 February 2007.
3 One major problem with *The Small Town* is the casting of professionals in the post-dubbing process. Ceylan says that he could not shoot the film with sync-sound, since he had a cheap low-quality camera that sounded like a machine-gun during the shooting. Having amateurs dubbed by professional actors creates an artificial effect. Geoff Andrew, 'Beyond the Clouds: An Interview with Nuri Bilge Ceylan,' *Senses of Cinema* (June 2004), http://www.sensesofcinema.com/contents/04/32/nuri_bilge_ceylan.html. Accessed 20 January 2007.
4 Ceylan's approach to the province is clearly different from that of popular nostalgia films in the sense that he does not project a

romanticized image of collective childhood onto his provincial settings. Rather than being an imaginary site of innocence and purity, the province in Ceylan's cinema is an ambivalent space where we can observe paradoxes of belonging in contemporary Turkish society. A similar image of the province is to be found also in several other new wave films. *Boats Out of Watermelon Rinds* (*Karpuz Kabuğundan Gemiler Yapmak*, Ahmet Uluçay, 2004), *Times and Winds* (*Beş Vakit*, Reha Erdem, 2006), *Egg* (*Yumurta*, Semih Kaplanoğlu, 2007), and *Summer Book* (*Tatil Kitabı*, Seyfi Teoman, 2008) can be cited among the most interesting examples of the films whose approach to the province recalls Ceylan's cinema.

5 'From *Kasaba* to *Uzak*: Interview with Nuri Bilge Ceylan,' *Turkishtime* 16 (May–June 2003), www.turkishtime.org. Accessed 23 July 2005.

6 The perception of Turkey's status as provincial in relation to the Western world is a widely held view in Turkey. Nobel-winning author Orhan Pamuk, for example, voices a similar view. For the past 200 years, he maintains, an immense attempt has been made to occidentalize Turkey. 'I believe in that,' says Pamuk, 'but once your culture thinks of itself as weak, and tries to copy another, you sense that the center is some place else. Being non-western is the feeling that you are at the periphery.' Reported by Maya Jaggi, 'Between Two Worlds,' *Guardian*, 8 December 2007, http://books.guardian. co.uk/print/0,,331488423-99931,00.html. Accessed 20 January 2008.

7 Elsewhere I have examined the theme of provinciality in *Distant* in relation to Hamid Naficy's (2001) concept of 'accented cinema' (Suner, 2006).

8 Howard Feinstein, 'Nuri Bilge Ceylan Talks About the Truths of Distant,' *Indiewire* 9 (March 2004), http://www.nbcfilm.com/uzak/press_indiewirehoward.php. Accessed 20 January 2007.

9 Jason Wood, 'A Quick Chat with Nuri Bilge Ceylan,' *Kamera* 224 (May 2004), http://www.nbcfilm.com/uzak/press_kamerainterview. php. Accessed 20 January 2008.

10 Geoff Andrew, 'Beyond the Clouds: An Interview with Nuri Bilge Ceylan,' *Senses of Cinema*, June 2004, http://www.sensesofcinema. com/contents/04/32/nuri_bilge_ceylan.html. Accessed 20 January 2007.

11 Ibid.

12 Ibid.

13 Anthony Lane, 'Men's Secrets: *Distant* and *The Return*,' *The New Yorker*, 15 March 2004.
14 Reported by S.F. Said, 'Modern Master in the Old Style,' *Daily Telegraph*, 21 March 2004, http://www.nbcfilm.com/uzak/press_dailytelegraphsaid.php. Accessed 20 January 2008.

CHAPTER 4

1 Unpublished interview conducted in Istanbul in October 2002.
2 Fiachra Gibbson, 'Jail Made Me a Film Director,' *Guardian*, 30 January 2006, http://film.guardian.co.uk/print/0,,5386742-3181,00. html. Accessed 22 February 2008.
3 Although several sources cite *Waiting Room* as the third film of the 'Tales of Darkness' trilogy (since it was made after *Fate* and *Confession*, the first two films of the series), Demirkubuz himself has said that he has not yet completed his trilogy. The story that he considered the final part of this trilogy, a film called *Hicran*, has never been made. An extraordinarily candid person, Demirkubuz has admitted that he regrets having come up with the idea of a trilogy in the first place. Since all of his films explore the malicious side of human nature, they all are about darkness. Thus it would not be meaningful to single out three of them and designate them as 'tales of darkness' (Demirkubuz, 2006: 8).
4 Fiachra Gibbson, 'Jail Made Me a Film Director,' *Guardian*, 30 January 2006, http://film.guardian.co.uk/print/0,,5386742-3181,00. html. Accessed 22 February 2008.
5 Nadir Öperli and Fırat Yücel, interview with Zeki Demirkubuz, *Altyazı* 56 (November 2006), http://www.altyazi.net/kasim06/zeki. html. Accessed 22 February 2008.
6 Ibid.
7 Apart from the lines repeated between the two films, there are also repeated visual elements noticed by observant audiences. Özlem Köksal, for example, observes that Bekir in *Destiny* wears the same jacket that Yusuf wears in *Innocence*. Özlem Köksal, 'Kameranın Ahlakı (Interview with Zeki Demirkubuz),' *Express*, April 2007.
8 The term 'fate' is often defined as an outcome determined by an outside agency acting upon a person, while the term 'destiny' implies that the person is willfully participating in achieving an outcome. Demirkubuz himself indicates that *yazgı*, the Turkish word for fate, connotes something more modern and intellectual,

while *kader*, the Turkish word for destiny, sounds more 'Eastern.' Nadir Öperli and Fırat Yücel, interview with Zeki Demirkubuz, *Altyazı* 56 (November 2006), http://www.altyazi.net/kasim06/zeki. html. Accessed 22 February 2008.

 9 Unpublished interview conducted in Istanbul in October 2002.

10 Demirkubuz made these comments at the Paso Students Film Festival at Bilkent University, Ankara, 22 April 2005.

11 According to Michel Chion (1999), the counterpart of *acousmêtre* in cinema is the figure of the mute. It would be interesting, in this sense, to read the position of the two mute female characters in *Innocence* in relation to the use of acousmatic sound in *The Third Page*.

12 Unpublished interview conducted in Istanbul in October 2002.

CHAPTER 5

 1 Zaim uses this expression in another interview. See David Walsh, 'Interview with Dervis Zaim, Director of *Somersault in a Coffin'*, 20 October 1997, http://tcnarchive.blogspot.com/2007/09/interview-with-dervis-zaim-on.html. Acessed 24 January 2008.

 2 Defined as a 'spatial disease' first diagnosed during the late nineteenth century in modern metropolises, agoraphobia is an outcome of urban experience. The symptoms of agoraphobia (sensations of heat, blushing, trembling, and so forth) are exacerbated by the dimensions of the space, especially when there seems to be no boundary to the visual field (Vidler, 1991: 35).

 3 Hagia Sophia, one of the most important historical sites of Istanbul, is a former patriarchal basilica, which after the Ottoman conquest was turned into a mosque, and after the establishment of the Republic into a museum.

 4 While the screenplay of *Istanbul Tales* is written by Ümit Ünal, one of the most prolific writers of Turkish cinema since the 1980s, each fairytale adaptation was shot by a different director: Ümit Ünal (The Pied Piper), Kudret Sabancı (Snow White), Selim Demirdelen (Cinderella), Yücel Yolcu (Sleeping Beauty), and Ömür Atay (Little Red Riding Hood). Mehmet Aksın worked as a cinematographer on all five stories.

 5 http://www.anlatistanbul.com/english/default.asp. Accessed 24 January 2008.

 6 Film critics often mention *Birds of Exile* (*Gurbet Kuşları*, Halit Refiğ, 1964) as the first critically acclaimed film on the problem of internal

migration that reflects the perspective of the newcomers to the city. Feride Çiçekoğlu (2007) suggests that *Nights of Istanbul* (*Istanbul Geceleri*, Mehmet Muhtar, 1950) is actually the first film that looks at Istanbul through the eyes of the provincial characters.

7 It is interesting to note that after the international success of the film both German and Turkish media claimed *Head-On* for their own nations respectively. Following the 2004 Berlin Film Festival, where the film won the Golden Bear award, German newspapers hailed the film as part of German cinema and the first German film to receive the Golden Bear after some eighteen years, while Turkish newspapers celebrated the 'great victory' of a 'Turkish filmmaker.' It was not difficult, however, to detect an element of confusion in the air of applause, arising from not exactly knowing what to do with Akın's film. *Head-On*, after all, was a film resisting easy classification into given categories, frameworks, or cultural clichés. For this reason, following the publicity produced by the award ceremony in Berlin, most media coverage in both Germany and Turkey focused not so much on the film itself, but rather on the controversies and scandals involving the performers. For a discussion of the film from the perspective of German cinema, see Burns (2007) and Nicodemus (2007).

8 Wendy Mitchell, interview with Fatih Akın, 'Going to Extremes: Fatih Akın on His Turkish-German Love Story *Head-On*,' *Turkish Cinema Newsletter*, 20 April 2005, http://turkfilm.blogspot.com/search?q=going+to+extremes. Accessed 27 January 2008.

9 Ibid.

10 Elsewhere I have attempted to read the meaning of the musical sequences in *Head-On* in relation to the lyrics of several Turkish popular songs used in the film (Suner, 2005). One persistent motif in these songs is that of *kara sevda*, a notion that could be translated as 'dark passion.' As a prevailing motif in many fables and myths of the East, as well as in Turkish music, cinema, folk songs, folk tales, and poetry, dark passion points to an overwhelming emotional condition, one that is experienced almost like an incurable illness. Usually referring to doomed love affairs, 'dark' turns into a condemning idiom signifying suffering inflicted by passion. Those who fall into dark passion cannot possibly recover; they will forever be transformed by it. Despite its seemingly disheartening connotations, there also lies a subtle promise in dark passion: it provides one with a certain kind of

191

wisdom, a deeper insight of life. It teaches one to be courageous enough to risk everything for love, yet it also teaches to accept defeat. It inflicts pain, yet it gives the strength to endure it. Dark passion, in this sense, is both poison and remedy at once. The bizarre bond between Cahit and Sibel in *Head-On* resembles very much a dark passion of this sort. Fatih Akın emphasizes that the sensibility that we encounter in Turkish music is also found in Western punk music: 'Both are about how you can love somebody so much you go insane, you feel so much passion that you want to hurt yourself. Even with Depeche Mode or Nick Cave or Iggy Pop, I discovered a connection to the Eastern world, so I wanted to bring that to the film.' Wendy Mitchell, interview with Fatih Akın, 'Going to Extremes: Fatih Akın on His Turkish-German Love Story *Head-On*,' *Turkish Cinema Newsletter*, 20 April 2005, http://turkfilm.blogspot.com/search?q=going+to+extremes. Accessed 27 January 2008.

11 Brenna MacCrimmon and Selim Sesler. *Karşılama* (CD), Kalan, 1998.

12 Having grown up in Germany and being of Turkish origin, the protagonists of *Head-On* seem to feel themselves equally (not) at home in both Turkish and German cultures. They freely quote from their Turkish and German cultural heritages alike. The film approaches this situation not as a problem of non-belonging, but rather as an opportunity to construct multiple belongings. Instead of portraying the experience of exile in terms of homelessness and loss, *Head-On* emphasizes its enabling side. Multi-linguality and accented speech, in this regard, constitute a crucial aspect of *Head-On*. Turkish-German characters in the film continuously move between languages when they speak with each other. Cahit and Sibel speak both German and Turkish with a heavy accent. Time and again, the continuous moving between languages turns into an ironic, and at times subversive, element in the film (Suner, 2005).

13 Feride Çiçekoğlu, 'The Sound of Istanbul: 1950–2004,' presented at Orienting Istanbul: Cultural Capital of Europe?, University of California, Berkeley. 25–7 September 2008.

14 Catherine Simpson, 'Turkish Cinema's Resurgence: The "Deep Nation" Unravels,' *Senses of Cinema*, 2006, http://www.sensesofcinema.com/contents/06/39/turkish_cinema.html. Accessed 24 January 2008.

15 The old photographs of Istanbul in *Crossing the Bridge* are acquired from Ara Gürel's archive, a world-famous Turkish photographer of Armenian origin.

16 Among the prominent examples of the new wave Turkish films that tell their stories against the backdrop of Istanbul, we can cite *Mommy, I'm Scared* (*Korkuyorum Anne*, Reha Erdem, 2004), *Derivative* (*Türev*, Ulaş İnan İnaç, 2005), and *Two Girls* (*İki Genç Kız*, Kutluğ Ataman, 2005). *Turkish Bath* (*Il Bagno Turco/Hamam*, 1997) and *Harem Suaré* (1999), films by Turkish director Ferzan Özpetek, who resides and works in Italy, can also be considered as part of the emerging transnational genre of Istanbul films.

17 A similar argument is made by Ackbar Abbas (1997) in relation to the representation of the city of Hong Kong in new wave Hong Kong films.

CHAPTER 6

1 Semire Ruken Öztürk has estimated that the total number of women directors making feature-length films in Turkish film history is twenty-three. The total number of films that they have made so far is less than 100, among the more than 6,000 films produced in Turkish cinema (Öztürk, 2006: 58).

2 In the final days of writing this book, woman director Handan İpekçi's feature film on honor killings, *Hidden Faces* (*Saklı Yüzler*, 2007), was released.

3 'Oyun,' *Turkish Cinema Newsletter*, http://turkfilm.blogspot.com/search?q=pelin+esmer. Accessed 1 February 2008.

4 Eylem Kaftan's words are quoted in '*Vendetta Song*,' Boloji.com, http://www.boloji.com/wfs3/wfs388.htm. Accessed 12 March 2009.

5 Eylem Kaftan has suggested that the resemblance of the Turkish title of her film to Atıf Yılmaz's *Vasfiye Is Her Name* came as a surprise to her. She contends that she chose this title to record in history the name, identity, and life of a woman who is deprived even of a gravestone of her own. Unpublished interview conducted in Istanbul on 13 February 2008.

AFTERWORD

1 Quoted by Adorno from Friedrich Nietzsche, *Werke* (ed. Schlechta), Munich 1955, vol. II: 154 (English version in Friedrich Nietzsche, *The Joyful Wisdom*, Edinburgh and London, 1910: 203).
2 On the concept of ideology, Slavoj Zizek writes that 'there is no reality without the spectre' (Zizek, 2000: 21).

REFERENCES

Abbas, Ackbar. 1997. *Hong Kong: Culture and the Politics of Disappearence*. Minneapolis: University of Minnesota.

Abisel, Nilgün. 1994. *Türk Sineması Üzerine Yazılar*. Ankara: İmge.

Adorno, Theodor W. 2002 [first published 1951]. *Minima Moralia*, trans. E.F.N. Jephcott. London: Verso.

Ahıska, Meltem. 2003. 'Occidentalism: The Historical Fantasy of the Modern.' *South Atlantic Quarterly* 102 (2/3): 351–79.

Altınay, Ayşe Gül. 1999. '*Mehmedin Kitabı*: Challenging Narratives of War and Nationalism.' *New Perspectives on Turkey* 21: 125–45.

——. 2007. 'Ebru: Reflections on Water.' In *Ebru: Reflections of Cultural Diversity in Turkey*, ed. Ayşe Gül Altınay. Istanbul: Metis: 19–25.

Altınsay, İbrahim. 1996. 'Sinemanın Orta Yeri İstanbul'du.' *İstanbul* 18: 73–5.

Amireh, Amal and Lisa Suhair Majaj. 2000. 'Introduction.' In *Going Global: The Transnational Reception of Third World Women Writers*, ed. Amal Amireh and Lisa Suhair Majaj. New York: Garland Publishing: 1–26.

Bachelard, Gaston. 1994 [first published 1958]. *The Poetics of Space: The Classic Look at How We Experience Intimate Places*, trans. Maria Jolas. Boston: Beacon.

Bakhtin, Mikhail. 1984. *Problems of Dostoevski's Poetics*, trans. Caryl Emerson. Minneapolis: University of Minnesota Press.

Bal, Mieke. 1999. 'Introduction.' In *Acts of Memory: Cultural Recall in the Present*, ed. Mieke Bal, Jonathan Crewe, and Leo Spitzer. Hanover and London: Dartmouth College: vii–xvii.

Balibar, Etienne. 1992. 'Class Racism.' In *Race, Nation and Class: Ambigious Identities*, ed. Etienne Balibar and Immanuel Wallerstein, trans. Chris Turner. London and New York: Verso.

Baydar, Gülsüm and Berfin İvegen. 2006. 'Territories, Identities, and Tresholds: The Saturday Mothers Phenomenon in Istanbul.' *Signs: Journal of Women in Culture and Society* 31 (3): 689–715.

Bell, Vikki. 1999. 'Performativity and Belonging: Introduction.' *Theory, Culture and Society* 16 (2): 1–10.

Berry, Chris 2006. 'Zeki Demirkubuz: By the Light of the Dark.' Translated and published in *Kader: Zeki Demirknuz*, ed. Samire Ruken Öztürk. Ankara: Dost: 19-25.

Bora, Tanıl. 2003. 'Nationalist Discourses in Turkey.' *South Atlantic Quarterly* 102 (2/3): 433–51.

Boym, Svetlana. 2001. *The Future of Nostalgia*. New York: Basic Books.

Brison, Susan J. 1999. 'Trauma Narratives and the Remaking of the Self.' In *Acts of Memory: Cultural Recall in the Present*, ed. Mieke Bal, Jonathan Crewe, and Leo Spitzer. Hanover and London: Dartmouth College: 39–54.

Burns, Rob. 2007. 'Towards a Cinema of Cultural Hybridity: Turkish-German Filmmakers and the Representation of Alterity.' *Debatte: Journal of Contemporary Central and Eastern Europe* 15 (1): 3–24.

Büker, Seçil. 2002. 'The Film Does Not End with an Ecstatic Kiss.' In *Fragments of Culture: The Everyday of Modern Turkey*, ed. Deniz Kandiyoti and Ayşe Saktanber. New Brunswick, NJ: Rutgers University Press: 147–70.

Calvino, Italo. 1974. *Invisible Cities*, trans. William Weaver. New York: Harvest Books.

Ceylan, Nuri Bilge. 2003. *Mayıs Sıkıntısı*. Istanbul: Norgunk.

——. 2004. *Uzak*. Istanbul: Norgunk.

Chaudhuri, Shohini and Howard Finn. 2003. 'The Open Image: Poetic Realism and the New Iranian Cinema.' *Screen* 44 (1): 38–57.

Chion, Michel. 1999. *The Voice in Cinema*, trans. Claudia Gorbman. New York: Columbia University Press.

Çiçekoğlu, Feride. 2007. *Vesikalı Şehir*. Istanbul: Metis.

Dabashi, Hamid. 2001. *Close-Up Iranian Cinema: Past, Present and Future*. London: Verso.

De Lauretis, Teresa. 1984. *Alice Doesn't: Feminism, Semiotics and Cinema*. London: Macmillan.

——. 1990. 'Eccentric Subjects: Feminist Theory and Historical Consciousness.' *Feminist Studies* 16 (1): 115–50.

Deleuze, Gilles. 1989. *Cinema 2: The Time-Image*, trans. Hugh Tomlinson and Robert Galeta. Minneapolis: University of Minnesota Press.

REFERENCES

Demirkubuz, Zeki. 2006. 'Her Filmimi Büyük Bir Aşağılanma Duygusu İçinde Çekiyorum.' In *Sinema Söyleşileri: Boğaziçi Üniversitesi Mithat Alam Film Merkezi Söyleşi, Panel ve Sunum Yıllığı 2005*, ed. Gülhan Düzgün and Yamaç Okur. Istanbul: Boğaziçi Üniversitesi Yayınevi: 3–24.

Dorsay, Atilla. 2004. *Sinemamızda Çöküş ve Rönesans Yılları*. Istanbul: Remzi.

Duben, Alan. 2007. 'A Fluidity of Identities.' In *Ebru: Reflections of Cultural Diversity in Turkey*, ed. Ayşe Gül Altınay. Istanbul: Metis: 64–5.

Durak, Attila. 2007. 'Artist's Statement.' In *Ebru: Reflections of Cultural Diversity in Turkey*, ed. Ayşe Gül Altınay. Istanbul: Metis: 13–14.

Erdoğan, Nezih. 1998. 'Narratives of Resistance: National Identity and Ambivalence in the Turkish Melodrama between 1965 and 1975.' *Screen* 39 (3): 259–71.

——. 2002. 'Mute Bodies, Disembodied Voices: Notes on Sound in Turkish Popular Cinema.' *Screen* 43 (3): 233–49.

Erdoğan, Nezih and Deniz Göktürk. 2001. 'Turkish Cinema.' In *Companion Encyclopedia of Middle Eastern and North African Film*, ed. Oliver Leaman. New York: Routledge: 533–67.

Ezra, Elizabeth and Terry Rowden. 2006. 'General Introduction: What is Transnational Cinema?' In *Transnational Cinema: The Film Reader*, ed. Elizabeth Ezra and Terry Rowden. London and New York: Routledge: 1–12.

Freud, Sigmund. 2003 [first published 1919]. 'The Uncanny.' In *The Uncanny*, trans. David McLintock. New York: Penguin Books: 121–61.

Göktürk, Deniz. 2008. 'Sound Bridges: Transnational Mobility as Ironic Drama.' In *Shifting Landscapes: Film and Media in European Context*, ed. Miyase Christensen and Nezih Erdoğan. Cambridge: Cambridge Scholars Press: 153–71.

Gürbilek, Nurdan. 1995. *Yer Değiştiren Gölge*. Istanbul: Metis.

——. 1999. *Ev Ödevi*. Istanbul: Metis.

——. 2001. *Kötü Çocuk Türk*. Istanbul: Metis.

Hall, Stuart. 1994. 'Cultural Identity and Diaspora.' In *Colonial Discourse and Post-Colonial Theory: A Reader*, ed. Patrick Williams and Laura Chrisman. New York: Columbia University Press: 392–403.

Hayward, Susan. 1996. *Key Concepts in Cinema Studies*. London and New York: Routledge.

———. 2000. 'Framing National Cinemas.' In *Cinema and Nation*, ed. Mette Hjort and Scott MacKenzie. London and New York: Routledge: 88–102.

Higson, Andrew. 2000. 'The Limiting Imagination of National Cinema.' In *Cinema and Nation*, ed. Mette Hjort and Scott MacKenzie. London and New York: Routledge: 63–74.

Hung, Natalia Chan Sui. 2000. 'Rewriting History: Hong Kong Nostalgia Cinema and its Social Practice.' In *The Cinema of Hong Kong: History, Arts, Identity*, ed. David Desser and Poshek Fu. Cambridge: Cambridge University Press: 252–72.

Hutcheon, Linda. 1988. *A Poetics of Postmodernism: History, Theory, Fiction*. London and New York: Routledge.

———. 1989. *The Politics of Postmodernism*. London and New York: Routledge.

———. 1994. *Irony's Edge: The Theory and Politics of Irony*. London and New York: Routledge.

Huyssen, Andreas. 1995. *Twilight Memories: Marking Time in a Culture of Amnesia*. London and New York: Routledge.

———. 2003. *Present Pasts: Urban Palimpsests and the Politics of Memory*. Stanford, CA: Stanford University Press.

Jameson, Fredric. 1983. 'Postmodernism and Consumer Society.' In *The Anti-Aesthetic: Essays on Postmodern Culture*, ed. Hal Foster. Seattle: Bay Press: 111–25.

———. 1991. 'Nostalgia for the Present.' In *Postmodernism or the Cultural Logic of Late Capitalism*. Durham, NC: Duke University Press: 279–96.

Kandiyoti, Deniz. 2002. 'Introduction: Reading the Fragments.' In *Fragments of Culture: The Everyday of Modern Turkey*, ed. Deniz Kandiyoti and Ayşe Saktanber. New Brunswick, NJ: Rutgers University Press: 1–24.

Kasaba, Reşat. 1997. 'Kemalist Certainties and Modern Ambiquities.' In *Rethinking Modernity and National Identity in Turkey*, ed. Sibel Bozdoğan and Reşat Kasaba. Washington, DC: University of Washington Press: 15–36.

Kaya Mutlu, Dilek. 2007. 'The Russian Monument at Ayastefanos (San Stefano): Between Defeat and Revenge, Remembering and Forgetting.' *Middle Eastern Studies* 43 (1): 75–86.

Keyder, Çağlar. 1999. 'The Setting.' In *Istanbul Between the Global and the Local*, ed. Çağlar Keyder. Lanham, MD: Rowman and Littlefield: 3–28.

——. 2004. 'The Turkish Bell Jar.' *New Left Review* 28: 65–84.

Kurban, Dilek. 2007. 'Introduction to English Edition.' In *Coming to Terms with Forced Migration: Post-Displacement Restitution of Citizenship Rights in Turkey*, ed. Dilek Kurban et al . Istanbul: TESEV: 17–20.

Maktav, Hilmi. 2001/2. 'Türk Sinemasında Yeni Bir Dönem.' *Birikim* 152: 225–33.

Marks, Laura U. 2000. *The Skin of the Film: Intercultural Cinema, Embodiment and the Senses*. Durham, NC: Duke University Press.

Mater, Nadire. 1999. *Mehmedin Kitabı: Güneydoğu'da Savaşmış Askerler Anlatıyor*. Istanbul: Metis.

Monceau, Nicolas. 2001. 'Confronting Turkey's Social Realities: An Interview with Yeşim Ustaoğlu.' *Cineaste* 26 (3): 28–30.

Mulvey, Laura. 1989. *Visual Pleasure and Narrative Cinema*. London: Macmillan.

——. 2006. 'Abbas Kiarostami: Cinema of Uncertainty, Cinema of Delay.' In *Death 24x a Second: Stillness and the Moving Image*. London: Reaktion Books: 123–43.

Naficy, Hamid. 1996. 'Phobic Spaces and Liminal Panics: Independent Transnational Film Genre.' In *Global/Local: Cultural Production and the Transnational Imaginary*, ed. Rob Wilson and Wimal Dissanayake. Durham, NC: Duke University Press: 119–44.

——. 2001. *An Accented Cinema: Exilic and Diasporic Filmmaking*. Princeton: Princeton University Press.

Neyzi, Leyla. 2002. 'Remembering to Forget: Sabbateanism, National Identity, and Subjectivity in Turkey.' *Society for Comparative Study of Society and History* 44 (1): 137–58.

Nicodemus, Katja. 2007. 'Getting Real.' In *Germany in Transit: Nation and Migration, 1955–2005*, ed. Deniz Göktürk, David Gramling, and Anton Kaes. Berkeley: University of California Press: 465–8.

Öncü, Ayşe. 1997. 'The Myth of the "Ideal Home" Travels Across Cultural Borders to Istanbul.' In *Space, Culture and Power: New Identities in Globalizing Cities*, ed. Ayşe Öncü and Petra Weyland. London: Zed Book: 56–72.

Özön, Nijat. 1995. *Karagözden Sinemaya: Türk Sineması ve Sorunları 1. Cilt*. Ankara: Kitle Yayınları.

Öztürk, Semire Ruken. 2004. *Sinemanın Dişil Yüzü: Türkiye'de Kadın Yönetmenler*. Istanbul: Om Sinema.

——. 2006. 'Onlar Cinsiyet Olarak Kadın Yönetmen, Ama Aslında Erkek Olmayan Kadınlar.' In *Sinema Söyleşileri: Boğaziçi Üniversitesi Mithat Alam Film Merkezi Söyleşi, Panel ve Sunum Yıllığı 2005*,

ed. Gülhan Düzgün and Yamaç Okur. Istanbul: Boğaziçi Üniversitesi
Yayınevi: 53–69.
Öztürkmen, Arzu. 2006. 'Remembering Conflicts in a Black Sea Town:
A Multi-sited Ethnography of Memory.' *New Perspectives on Turkey*
34: 93–115.
Özyürek, Esra. 2007. 'Introduction: The Politics of Public Memory in
Turkey.' In *The Politics of Public Memory in Turkey*, ed. Esra Özyürek.
New York: Syracuse University Press: 1–15.
Pamuk, Orhan. 2005. *Istanbul: Memories and the City*, trans. Maureen
Freely. London: Faber and Faber.
Papastergiadis, Nikos. 1998. 'Introduction: The Home in Modernity.' In
Dialogues in the Diasporas: Essays and Conversations on Cultural Identity.
London and New York: Rivers Oram Press: 1–15.
Parla, Jale. 2003. 'Car Narratives: A Subgenre in Turkish Novel Writing.'
South Atlantic Quarterly 102 (2/3): 535–50.
Robins, Kevin and Asu Aksoy. 2000. 'Deep Nation: The National
Question and Turkish Cinema Culture.' In *Cinema and Nation*,
ed. Mette Hjort and Scott MacKenzie. London and New York:
Routledge: 203–21.
Shohat, Ella. 2003. 'Post-Third-Worldist Culture: Gender, Nation and
the Cinema.' In *Rethinking Third Cinema*, ed. Anthony R. Guneratne
and Wimal Dissanayake. London and New York: Routledge: 51–78.
Suner, Asuman. 1998. 'Speaking the Experience of Political Oppression
with a Masculine Voice: Making Feminist Sense of Yılmaz Güney's
The Way.' *Social Identities* 4 (2): 283–300.
——. 2002. 'Nostalgia for an Imaginary Home: Memory, Space and
Identity in New Turkish Cinema.' *New Perspectives on Turkey* 27:
61–76.
——. 2004. 'Horror of a Different Kind: Dissonant Voices of the New
Turkish Cinema.' *Screen* 45 (4): 305–23.
——. 2005. 'Dark Passion: Fatih Akın's *Head-On*.' *Sight and Sound* 15
(3): 18–21.
——. 2006. 'Outside In: Accented Cinema at Large.' *Inter-Asia Cultural
Studies* 7 (3): 361–80.
——. 2007. 'Cinema Without Frontiers: Transnational Women's
Filmmaking in Iran and Turkey.' In *Transnational Feminism in Film
and Media*, ed. Katarzyna Marciniak, Aniko Imre, and Aine O'Healy.
London and New York: Palgrave Macmillian: 53–70.
Tekeli, Şirin. 1995. 'Women in Turkey in the 1980s.' In *Women in Modern
Turkish Society*, ed. Şirin Tekeli. London: Zed Books: 1–22.

Vidler, Anthony. 1991. 'Agoraphobia: Spatial Estrangement in Georg Simmel and Siegfried Kracauer.' *New German Critique* 54: 31–45.

——. 1992. *The Architectural Uncanny: Essays in the Modern Unhomely*. Cambridge, MA: MIT Press.

Walker, Janet. 2005. *Trauma Cinema: Documenting Incest and the Holocaust*. Berkeley: University of California Press.

Waugh, Patricia. 1984. *Metafiction: The Theory and Practice of Self-Conscious Fiction*. New York: Routledge.

Winnicott, Donald, W. 1982. *Playing and Reality*. New York: Routledge.

Yücel, Fırat. 2005. 'İstanbul Hatırası: Doğaçlama Belgesel.' *Altyazı* 41: 44–5.

Zaim, Derviş. 2004. 'Sanat Tarihi Belirli Tercihlerin Tarihidir.' In *Sinema Söyleşileri: Boğaziçi Üniversitesi Mithat Alam Film Merkezi Söyleşi, Panel ve Sunum Yıllığı 2003*, ed. Berke Göl, Yamaç Okur, and Nadir Öperli. Istanbul: Boğaziçi Üniversitesi Yayınevi: 37–82.

Zizek, Slavoj. 2000. 'Introduction: The Spectre of Ideology.' In *Mapping Ideology*, ed. Slavoj Zizek. London and New York: Verso: 1–33.

INDEX